**2nd Australian &
New Zealand Edition**

Writing
Resumes &
Cover Letters

FOR

DUMMIES

A Wiley Brand

**by Amanda McCarthy
Kate Southam**

FOR

DUMMIES

A Wiley Brand

Writing Resumes & Cover Letters For Dummies®

2nd Australian and New Zealand Edition published by
Wiley Publishing Australia Pty Ltd
42 McDougall Street
Milton, Qld 4064
www.dummies.com

Copyright © 2014 Wiley Publishing Australia Pty Ltd

First edition published as *Australian Resumes For Dummies* © 2008 Wiley Publishing
Australia Pty Ltd.

The moral rights of the authors have been asserted.

National Library of Australia
Cataloguing-in-Publication data:

Author:	McCarthy, Amanda.
Title:	Writing Resumes & Cover Letters For Dummies / Amanda McCarthy, Kate Southam.
Edition:	2nd Australian and New Zealand ed.
ISBN:	9780730307808 (pbk.) 9780730307839 (ebook)
Series:	For Dummies.
Notes:	Includes index.
Subjects:	Resumes (Employment) — Australia. Resumes (Employment) — New Zealand. Applications for positions. Job hunting — Australia. Job hunting — New Zealand.
Other authors/ Contributors:	Kate Southam.
Dewey Number:	650.142

Cover image: © mediaphotos/iStockphoto.com

Typeset by diacriTech, Chennai, India

Printed in Singapore by
C.O.S. Printers Pte Ltd

10 9 8 7 6 5 4 3 2 1

Contents at a Glance

Table of Contents

Part II: Designing a Dazzling Resume 37

Chapter 3: Creating the Contents 39

Chapter 4: Winning Words for Resumes. 63

Part V: The Part of Tens........................253

Introduction

● ●

*C*hances are you're buying this book because you've never had to formally apply for a job during your long career and haven't a clue how to create a resume. Or maybe you're new to the world of work, re-entering the workforce after some time out or you're looking to change careers or just find a new job. Whatever your reason, you need to be congratulated for taking the initiative and investing in your career!

Writing Resumes & Cover Letters For Dummies, 2nd Australian and New Zealand Edition, is full of simple, practical ideas to help you create a standout resume and cover letter that grabs attention and gets you shortlisted for interview. We've been in the employment game for many years and have both helped people create winning resumes and cover letters. We also have a pretty good idea of what employers and recruitment consultants like and don't like. In this book you discover how to format your resume for ease of reading and get up to speed with resume trends, including ensuring your resume can be found easily when posted on the internet. You also get information on writing a cover letter that's sure to grab attention.

We're often amazed by people who send out their resumes here, there and everywhere without thinking about whether they really want the job or are the right fit for the company's corporate culture. One of the most important pieces of advice we can give you before you even start pulling together a resume is to do a little homework on yourself. Know your strengths. List the skills, experience, qualifications, career highs and achievements that make you a great asset for any employer. You'll use this information time and again when crafting your standout resume and cover letter.

Good luck in your job hunt!

About This Book

The job recruitment world is a pretty competitive place. Recruiters are often on the receiving end of hundreds of applications. To make the cut, your resume and cover letter need to jump out from the pile, create buzz and scream 'perfect match' to the employer's wish-list of skills and qualifications they want their new hire to have.

This book is packed with information, tips, tools and techniques to help you write a standout resume and accompanying cover letter that will set you apart from the competition. Whether you're new to the game of writing resumes and cover letters or looking to give your old resume a facelift, *Writing Resumes & Cover Letters For Dummies*, 2nd Australian and New Zealand Edition, will be a valuable addition to your bookshelf.

Foolish Assumptions

This book assumes you have a basic knowledge and understanding of the following:

- ✔ **Computer basics.** You know how to use a mouse and keyboard, and are familiar with basic computer terminology (that is, you know a virus is not just the flu and a mouse is not just a creature that eats cheese).

- ✔ **Email.** You know how to send and receive emails.

- ✔ **The internet.** You know how to navigate the web and use search engines.

- ✔ **Word-processing software.** You know how to open, close, save, create, print and edit documents. You have used the spellcheck function in your word-processing program and have inserted headers and footers.

Icons Used in This Book

In the left margins of the book, we use a number of icons to draw your attention to key points in the text. Following is a list of all the icons and what they mean:

Get your highlighter pen ready — this information is important and should not be forgotten.

Smart ideas to get your resume noticed.

This icon provides you with handy hints and useful suggestions to get your resume in shape.

Pay attention to this icon because it alerts you to any dangers, traps or potential pitfalls that may lie ahead. In other words, proceed with caution.

Beyond the Book

In addition to the information we share in this print or ebook, *Writing Resumes & Cover Letters For Dummies*, 2nd Australian and New Zealand Edition, also comes with some access-anywhere goodies available on the internet. Check out the free Cheat Sheet at www.dummies.com/cheatsheet/ writingresumescoverlettersau for some quick, helpful tips on creating your resume and cover letter. For additional companion material to this book, visit www.dummies.com/ extras/writingresumescoverlettersau.

Where to Go from Here

This book is a handy reference guide you can turn to again and again when you need specific resume help. Each chapter stands alone, which means you don't need to read the entire book in sequence — unless, of course, you want to! If you want, you can flick through the table of contents at the front of the book and zip straight to the sections that interest you most. For example, if your burning desire is to find out about what to include in your resume, go to Chapter 3. If you want to check out how to create a winning application for a government job, read Chapter 13. For the lowdown on cover letters, flick to Chapter 7, and if sample resumes are what you're after then see Chapter 10.

If you're fresh out of school or uni, we look at tailoring your resume and cover letter to maximum effect in Chapters 11 and 12.

Perhaps you want to know more about creating a social media profile that reinforces your resume pitch as the right person for the job — if so, flip to Chapter 8 to discover more about the benefits of using social media (and the potential pitfalls).

Wherever you begin, we wish you the best of luck with your resume and cover letter creation — we hope it wins you your dream job!

Part I
Getting Started with Creating Resumes and Cover Letters

getting started
with

resumes
and cover

letters

Visit www.dummies.com for great content online.

In this part...

✔ Explore the qualities of a winning resume and cover letter, work out what to include in your resume, and how to quickly impress an employer or recruiter.

✔ Choose the perfect resume format to showcase your potential and complement your work history.

Chapter 1

Introducing the First-Rate Resume and Cover Letter

A resume is more than just a piece of paper. It's a marketing document promoting a very important product — you. Your resume advertises your skills: You know you're a star and you know you can do the job; now you just need to prove this to the recruiter or employer. When it comes to jobs, you have plenty of competition out there. Your resume and cover letter need to be the ones that jump out of the pile, grab attention and land you an interview.

Putting together a revealing resume and a captivating cover letter takes time, effort and energy — they're not something that can be rushed. In this book, we share our experience and provide plenty of inside information based on years of talking to employers and recruitment consultants about what they're looking for when they review your resume and cover letter. Today, you need to tailor your resume and cover letter to each job you apply for. Recruiters and employers know how to spot a 'one size fits all' application. Employers want to believe you understand the role they are advertising and really want to work for their organisation, and tailoring your application to each job helps you show this.

You can also use job boards to post your resume online so employers can find you. Creating a winning social media profile that aligns with the image you want to project to employers also supports your standout resume.

In this chapter, we take you through the basics — what a resume is, its purpose, the keywords to include in your resume, the value of a well-crafted cover letter and the importance of using social media to support your job-hunting efforts.

Realising the Value of a Top-Notch Resume

Whether you're interested in moving up the ranks or finding a new job, a well-crafted, top-notch resume can help you get to where you want to go.

A standout resume is a profile of who you are. The standout resume tells the recruiter or employer your career story. Your resume showcases your skills, abilities, qualifications, experience and personal attributes and ties all of these to the particular job you're going for. The job of a standout resume is to get you noticed and shortlisted for an interview.

Your standout resume needs to convince the recruiter or employer that you have what it takes to do the job on offer. The things that make employers look twice include

- ✔ **Showing how your skills and experience match the criteria for the job.** Relevancy is the name of the game. Your resume must demonstrate that you understand the company and the role, and have the skills and experience required.

  We show you how to craft a targeted resume in Chapter 2, and explore how you can use a cover letter as your calling card in Chapter 7.

- ✔ **Flaunting your achievements.** Including past successes or achievements from your past two or three roles is a great way to show how you add value to an organisation.

A standout resume sells rather than tells. Don't be afraid to big-note yourself in your resume. We talk about promoting your strengths in Chapter 3 and provide specialised advice for school leavers and graduates in Chapters 11 and 12, respectively.

✔ **Putting in industry experience.** Nothing beats real-life work experience in your field. Even better when you've worked for some impressive names.

✔ **Scoring high marks.** Your university, college or school results speak volumes. When your academic record is strong, highlight the fact you blitzed it through university or school with straight As. See Chapters 11 and 12 for ways to present academic achievements.

Your resume will be scanned by a human eye or by a piece of software and summed up as a winner or a dud in a matter of seconds. Here are a few simple things you can do to create a positive first impression:

✔ Make sure your resume is easy to read. Use a simple layout.

✔ Keep your resume to around two to three pages.

✔ Mimic the keywords used in job ads.

✔ Back up any claims you make with examples.

✔ Proofread your document carefully.

To come out on top, you need to know what recruiters like and dislike in a resume. We provide some examples of offending behaviour in Chapter 14 and share our top tips for creating a standout resume in Chapter 15.

Don't make claims in your resume you can't back up with real-life examples. Any exaggeration that's uncovered will cast doubt on your entire work history.

Planning Your Approach

Whether you're putting together your resume and cover letter for the first time or fixing up old versions, you need to take your time and plan out each area of the information you will include. The key is to know as much about your career history and achievements as you can and then promote these dazzling facts in your resume and cover letter.

Remembering that your resume is valuable real estate

Getting your resume into shape requires time, effort and energy. Here are a few reasons you should consider writing your own resume rather than asking a friend or a professional to do it:

- ✔ You know yourself better than anyone else.
- ✔ You get to call the shots in terms of layout and content.
- ✔ You're on a tight budget, so paying a pro isn't an option.

However, if you want to explore using a professional, do your homework by

- ✔ **Getting a recommendation.** Ask friends, family, colleagues and contacts if they have used a professional resume writer and can make a recommendation.

- ✔ **Use reputable professionals.** Browse the websites of the Career Development Association of Australia — www.cdaa.org.au — or the Career Development Association of New Zealand — www.cdanz.org.au — to find a resume writer. These organisations require their members to maintain high standards of knowledge and conduct.

Understanding your work history

Does your resume sell your strengths to a potential employer and promote you in the best possible light? Is your resume tailored to the job or are you using a generic document? Is your resume getting you results? Are you scoring interviews? If you answered 'no', it's time to revisit your career history.

You may think you're pretty good at selling yourself until you sit down at a computer with a blank Word document in front of you. Time to jog your memory, and dig out all the wonderful raw material stored in your head, as well as in old documents, letters and emails.

Start by jotting down where you worked, including the full company name and the month and year you started and finished each job. Reconstruct your day-to-day job tasks. Also recall any training you undertook and make a note of who you reported to in each job. List everything special that happened, such as a win for the team, any letters, notes or emails of praise you received and any awards you won. To help gather the information you need, consider these questions:

✓ **What were your responsibilities?** Write down the daily tasks you performed in each job. If you kept any of your old job descriptions or letters of offer, get them out and dust them off for details of your past work life.

✓ **What are your qualifications?** List degrees, trade qualifications, industry certifications and certificates of completion for training courses on everything from workplace safety to team building. Also make a note of the teaching institution or training company and the month and year you completed each course.

✓ **What are your transferable skills?** Make a note of all the skills that you could use in most jobs and how you developed these skills. Examples would be communication skills and proficiency using the most common software packages, such as Microsoft Office. This information will come in handy later when you are tailoring your resume and cover letter to each job application.

✓ **What are your biggest achievements?** Employers and recruiters believe that what you've done in the past is a good indication of what you'll do in the future if you're hired. Your responsibilities are the tasks you were paid to do, but your achievements demonstrate how you took a job and made it your own. We discuss achievements in detail in Chapter 3.

Start thinking now about the ways you demonstrated extra effort. Did you put forward a suggestion or idea that was adopted? What were the results? List any awards or commendations you received.

✓ **What are your key personal attributes?** Personal attributes are those qualities that make you stand out. What are the traits people compliment you on? What are you most proud of when you think of yourself as a good employee? Examples could be 'punctual', 'well presented', 'highly motivated', 'dynamic', 'results-driven', 'innovative', and 'proactive'.

✓ **Where are your past managers?** When it comes to reference checking, candidates, recruiters and employers prefer to talk to the managers and supervisors you reported to directly. Do you know how to contact your former managers? If you don't, use the internet, including social media, to find where your previous managers work now and how to contact them. You can also phone the main reception desk at the companies where you were previously employed to ask if a manager still works there and what their current title is. Don't leave this task to the last minute.

✔ **How can you stand out from the crowd?** When it comes to jobs, recruiters often wade through hundreds of applications. Your resume needs to stand out from the crowd. While you don't want to lie or pad your resume with half-baked truths, you need to lay claim to all your achievements and be prepared to sing your own praises.

Covering the essentials: The importance of your cover letter

Your resume may contain all the essential detail you need to present to a potential employer to win that interview, but your cover letter is the introduction that gets you noticed. If you have a strong cover letter, it increases the chance that your resume will be read through rather than glanced over.

Your cover letter complements your resume, presenting you as the ideal candidate who's well-matched to the role. It also provides you with the opportunity to demonstrate your understanding of the company's culture, and how you can add value to the organisation.

We look at cover letters in detail in Chapter 7, exploring the structure of your cover letter and how to target your approach. We also explore how school leavers can impress their first potential employer in Chapter 11, and consider how graduates can target their cover letter to different graduate opportunities in Chapter 12.

Supporting your resume: The role of social media

Creating a social media profile is almost a must these days, but employers and recruitment consultants want to see your resume too when considering you for a job. Your social media profile is an important support act for your resume — not a substitute.

Be known for all the right reasons

Getting the balance right can be tricky when using social media, so consider these tips to help you get the most out of your online presence:

✔ Use a professional-looking photo on your career-related profiles, preferably a head and shoulders shot. Avoid using holiday shots with casual clothes, or wedding shots with a spouse cropped out.

✔ Ask friends and family to de-tag you from unflattering photos or commentary on their own social media pages.

✔ Use maximum privacy settings for your Facebook page or remove anything that does not align to your professional image.

✔ Be warned: Some recruiters will ask for access to your social media pages, including Facebook. Take a breath before responding. You can always say that you only use Facebook for family and friends, and offer a link to your professional social media pages instead.

✔ Use Twitter to follow industry leaders in your field so you can tap into the latest trends and even expand your network.

LinkedIn is the best-known social media platform for the career-minded. Other useful social networks exist, including Google+, Facebook and Twitter, and we go into detail about how to create a positive and professional social media profile in Chapter 8.

Creating a Resume That Gets Noticed Online

The growth of the internet since the late 1990s has changed the way recruitment happens. Today, job seekers create and post resumes online, and both small and large companies and recruitment agencies are using online databases to store and retrieve, and search for, resumes (and, therefore, suitable candidates). Relevancy is the name of the game. Until the interview, you're more a collection of skills, experience, knowledge, education and training than a living and breathing person. Databases will be searched in a range of ways, including

- ✔ By a software program looking for particular skills and experience

- ✔ By a HR officer conforming to a strict list of criteria

- ✔ By a busy small-business employer who has posted a job ad and is scanning applicant resumes in a matter of seconds

- ✔ By a recruitment consultant who specialises in a particular area of a specific industry or professional sector

For all these reasons, stick to using commonly recognised words and terms in your resume.

Many employers and recruiters use software programs to search for resumes posted online. By using lots of useful keywords in your resume taken from a job ad or position description or simply mimicking the most commonly used terms in your sector to describe your skills, experience and qualifications, you increase the chances of your resume being selected by one of these programs.

Using keywords

How does a keyword search work? Say you're applying to a large recruitment agency for a job. You start off by sending the recruiter a copy of your resume, either by email or by posting it online via a job board or the consultant's own website. The recruiter has a quick look through the document, then places it into their computerised database for storage. These databases house millions of resumes. When a vacancy pops up that needs to be filled, the recruiter does a keyword search on all resumes in the database to retrieve the ones that match the job search criteria. The more keywords you have in your resume, the greater the chance your resume is 'picked up'.

Keywords are nouns or short phrases that the computer searches for. Keywords can be

- ✔ **Job titles:** For example, marketing coordinator, property manager or cabinet maker.

- ✔ **Skills and personal attributes:** Examples include organisational skills, communication skills and attention to detail.

- ✔ **Industry buzzwords, jargon or technical terms:** For example, a product manager may use the terms 'product development', 'marketing campaign' or 'search engine marketing' in a resume.

- ✔ **Computer software, hardware and languages:** For example, Microsoft Word, AutoCAD or Java/J2EE.

- ✔ **Education, qualifications and certificates:** An example is Certificate IV in Training and Assessment.

- ✔ **Languages:** Mandarin, Cantonese, Japanese and so on.

- ✔ **Professional certifications and licences:** For example, CPA or forklift licence.

Always be specific in your resume rather than general. For example, don't write 'Proficient in computer packages'; instead, say 'Proficient in Microsoft Word, Excel and Publisher'.

You can display keywords in your resume in lots of different ways, including

- ✔ A keyword summary at the beginning of your resume:

    Experienced **HR Manager** with a **Graduate Diploma of Human Resource Management** from Monash University.

    Expertise in recruitment, **training and development**, **performance management**, **industrial relations**, OHS and **succession planning**.

- ✔ A list of key skills. Presented as a list using dot points, the list of key skills reflects what the employer or recruiter has spelled out in the job ad using relevant keywords.

Alternatively, you can include keywords randomly throughout your resume.

If you don't have a clue where to find keywords for your occupation or industry, begin by trying these resources:

- ✔ **Hunt through job ads.** Look for keywords in newspaper and online advertisements. Use these keywords in your resume and cover letter — as long as you can genuinely lay claim to them.

- ✔ **Find a job description.** Highlight keywords in job descriptions and selection criteria.

✔ **Talk to industry professionals.** If you're moving into a new industry, get familiar with the terminology by talking to professionals already in the field.

✔ **Read industry and trade journals.** Pluck keywords out of industry magazines and journals.

✔ **Use LinkedIn.** The social media platform LinkedIn allows you to type in a job title and search through a list of the most commonly used words in job ads for that role.

In today's world of work, new job titles are springing up all the time, particularly in sectors featuring new technologies. Use the most common keywords in your resume rather than going for the unusual or unique titles and terms. Remember, you want to be found.

Being a 'creative ninja' instead of a public relations consultant or a 'manager of first impressions' instead of a receptionist might look great on a business card but it will not help a recruiter find your resume. At the very least, translate any whacky job title with its more commonly known counterpart.

We provide examples of keywords for different professions in Chapter 4.

Sending resumes as email attachments

One of the most popular ways to send a resume to a recruitment consultant or employer in Australia and New Zealand is via email. Sending your resume as an attachment enables you to retain the document's format. If you were to copy and paste your resume from your computer into the body of an email you may well mess up the formatting of the document. It may look okay from your end but from the recruiters, just the opposite — a garbled mess. You can also attach your cover letter to the same email as a separate document or include the cover letter as the first page on your resume document.

Here are some factors to consider when sending your resume as an email attachment:

✔ Always email your resume in the requested file format. If no specific instructions are mentioned in the job ad, ring the company or agency to see if they have a preference.

Otherwise play it safe and send your resume in a widely accepted format such as Microsoft Word. If you send your resume in an obscure word processing program, the recruiter may have trouble opening your attachment.

If you find the software program you use is incompatible with the recruiter's, consider saving your document in a universal file format such as Rich Text Format (RTF). You could save it as a PDF but check with the employer or recruiter first as many find PDFs inflexible when they want to edit your resume into their own internal format.

✔ When emailing your resume and cover letter in response to a particular advertisement, type the job title and reference number in the subject line of the email.

✔ Check that your attachment is virus-free. Viruses are commonly spread through opening email attachments. Safeguard yourself by installing anti-virus software on your computer, scanning files regularly for viruses and downloading the latest virus protection updates. You can choose from lots of different anti-virus programs on the market. Some of the more popular ones include Norton Antivirus (www.symantec.com), Trend Micro (www.trendmicro.com.au) and McAfee Antivirus (www.mcafee.com).

✔ Don't call your file name 'resume'. Hundreds of others may do the same. Instead name it 'Jessica Harris resume' or 'Harris, Jessica resume'.

✔ Before you click the Send button, check that the email address is correct and your resume is attached.

We offer additional tips on emailing your resume without incident in Chapter 6. We also cover polishing your resume so you can be confident it arrives with the recruiter in perfect shape.

Posting resumes on the web

Resume posting is simply placing your resume on an employment or company website for public viewing, so you can be headhunted for a job.

There's no right or wrong way to post your resume online. Each job site has its own instructions to follow.

No matter which method you use to get your resume online, consider these special factors:

✔ **Ease of use.** Go with sites that enable you to edit or remove your resume easily. Stay away from job boards that charge you a fee to use their website.

✔ **Password recollection.** Keep a record of all your usernames and passwords.

If you forget your log-in details, simply click on Forgotten Your Password, enter your email address and the system automatically emails your username and password to you.

✔ **Resume removal.** After you've landed a new job, remove your resume from the site.

✔ **Updates.** If your details change during the job-hunting process, update your entry. Keep your resume current.

✔ **Privacy statements.** A major drawback of resume posting is losing control over who sees your resume. Read through privacy statements on websites to see who can access your resume.

Register with websites that safeguard your privacy. Some sites allow you to hide your contact details or block certain employers (such as your current one) from viewing your resume.

Building your resume online

Some employers, job boards and industry websites invite you to build a resume online. This involves filling out set fields and/or using drop-down menus to populate an online resume template with relevant information about you. Many job boards invite you to simply upload your existing resume (see the previous section for more information). Employers and recruiters are then charged a fee to search a database of resumes, where they will hopefully find yours. Be sure to use plenty of keywords common to your job role, industry or profession to make it easy for employers and recruitment consultants to find you when they're searching for specific skillsets.

Here are three good reasons to build your resume online:

- ✔ **Easy to edit.** Adding and amending details is a cinch. You log in with your username and password, go to the relevant resume section that needs updating, and change the fields straightaway. Simple!

- ✔ **Get headhunted by hiring managers.** By clicking on the appropriate box when building your resume, you can either post your resume on their site for free or build a resume. You can choose to keep your current employer name a secret and even hide your own name making only your skills and experience visible.

- ✔ **Create and store multiple resumes.** Some high-tech websites enable you to create and store multiple resumes online.

A major limitation of online resume builders is their lack of flexibility. Sure, you can create, edit or even delete your own resumes, but changing the sequence of sections or adding additional headings to your resume is often difficult.

For more on keywords to include to help get your resume noticed online, flick to Chapter 4.

Chapter 2

Resume Formats to Fit You — and the Job

. . . .

In This Chapter

▶ Exploring the benefits of the reverse chronological order resume

▶ Considering alternative resume formats

▶ Tailoring your resume to a job or company

▶ Understanding the difference between a resume and a CV

. . . .

*Y*our resume markets a very important product — you. The primary purpose of your resume is to land you a job interview. From there, you can further sell yourself as the perfect person for the job.

The *format* of your resume is the way you arrange the content. The most commonly accepted format is the *reverse chronological order* resume, which lists your most recent experience first before moving back in time to your previous experience. Employers and recruitment consultants are able to run their eye down your resume and assess your work history at a glance.

In this chapter, we take a close look at the reverse chronological order resume, along with some alternative formats. In addition, we look at how to tailor your resume to target a specific job or company.

Lastly, we look at the differences between a curriculum vitae (CV) and a resume, and consider when using a CV may be more appropriate.

Starting from Today: The Reverse Chronological Order Resume

Recruiters and employers prefer the reverse chronological format — we show you an example in Figure 2-1. This type of resume lists your most recent work experience first and then works backwards in time. The same applies when listing your education and training. Using the reverse chronological order to lay out your resume enables recruitment consultants and hiring managers to see what is of most relevance to their hiring decision. This includes your job titles, company names, months and years of employment, responsibilities and achievements, listing your most recent experience first. By using this layout, employers can easily track your career to date at a glance. We provide details of other types of resumes too but the reverse chronological order resume is regarded as conventional and should be used in most circumstances.

Recruiters prefer dates of employment listed in months and years rather than just years. For example, write 'March 2010 – June 2013' instead of '2010 – 2013'. Be consistent with your approach and never use a mishmash of both — for example, '2010 – June 2013'.

Your work history should only go back about ten years. This may vary if you have only had one job during this time. In such cases, you could go back a little further. You can always include a section in your resume under the heading, 'Other Relevant Experience' to highlight any other outstanding job role or experience you have to offer. If you do include this additional section, omit the dates of employment. Creating this additional section is not about listing every job you've ever done but rather showcasing any useful skills acquired along the way, or top employers you've worked for.

The reverse chronological order resume has a number of advantages:

- ✔ The simple and easy-to-follow layout means recruiters don't have to dig deep to find your work history; it's spelt out clearly up front.

- ✔ You can highlight how your career has progressed from one job to the next.

- ✔ You can prove to the recruiter you have a stable work record.

- ✔ It's ideal if you're applying for jobs in conservative industries such as banking, finance, law and accounting.

Reverse Chronological Resume

Kate Martin

26 Greenview Drive   Mobile: 2222 222 222
Elizabeth Bay NSW 2011   Email: kmartin@email.com.au

Career Profile

A hands-on Product Manager with proven expertise in driving product lines, managing budgets, launching new products and developing marketing campaigns. Results-driven with a passion for achieving sales targets, increasing market share and boosting profits. I possess a strong business acumen and have well-developed communication, negotiation and project management skills. A strategic thinker with a positive 'can-do' attitude, I also hold a Masters of Marketing qualification.

Professional Experience

Product Manager (July 2008 – Present)
Equiptec Australia

Responsible for product management and marketing of Equiptec's fast-moving consumer range of all-in-one printers, laser printers, faxes, personal copiers and calculators.

Responsibilities:
- Manage the product-range mix planning and product lifecycle, including launch planning, marketing initiatives, stock management and end-of-life management.
- Develop and manage print, television and magazine advertising campaigns.
- Design and implement marketing materials, including brochures, catalogues, product portfolios and other retail point-of-sale devices in line with brand image and category marketing plan.
- Develop and execute product marketing plans and identify new growth opportunities through market research and competitor analysis.
- Product sales forecasting and inventory management.
- Manage a marketing budget in excess of $6 million.
- Attend head office meetings with major buying groups and conduct product knowledge training for sales staff.
- Supervise Marketing Coordinator.

Achievements:
- Doubled Equiptec's market share in the fast growing all-in-one printer market within 12 months through accurate stock procurement, creative promotional campaigns, aggressive advertising strategies, competitive pricing and effective channel management.
- Grew faster than market growth in mono laser printers and successfully launched Equiptec's first consumer colour laser printer on time and within budget.
- Increased sales by 80% through the implementation of consumer bonus campaigns.
- Expanded into new markets, generating $8m in revenue.
- Launched 24 new products in 2010 across 5 product categories, increasing sales by 10%.
- Achieved market leadership in combined inkjet printer market in 2011.

Figure 2-1: The reverse chronological resume—including a career profile (page 1 of 2).

2

Kate Martin
Professional Experience (continued)

Assistant Product Manager (February 2005 – June 2008)
Toshitsu

Responsibilities:
- Ensured the timely release of new products and managed all launch materials and requirements.
- Interacted with the Operations Department to organise shipping of incoming stock.
- Monitored and maintained inventory levels.
- Organised purchase orders to Tokyo and Malaysian Manufacturing plants.
- Reviewed and coordinated media schedule with advertising agency.
- Produced and distributed press releases for new products.
- Assisted in the promotion of dealer incentives.
- Compiled monthly competitive information bulletins for the sales team.

Achievements:
- Streamlined procurement processes, which increased efficiency and reduced errors by more than 50%.

Education
Master of Business Administration (2010)
University of Technology, Sydney

Bachelor of Commerce, Major in Marketing (2004)
Macquarie University

Memberships
- Australian Marketing Institute (AMI)
- Australian Institute of Management (AIM)

Referees
Available on request.

Figure 2-1: Continued (page 2 of 2).

The disadvantages of this format are:

- ✔ Job gaps or breaks in employment are easily spotted.
- ✔ Recruiters can readily figure out your age, particularly if your work experience is lengthy.
- ✔ Attention is drawn to the fact you've stayed in one position too long.

Other Types of Resume Formats

Although most employers expect to see the reverse chronological order resume format, at times you'll need to take a different approach. Fortunately, a couple of alternative resume styles exist that deliver the detail you need in certain circumstances:

- ✔ **Functional resume.** Focuses on your skills and downplays your work history. This style is used by those changing careers and job hunters that have inadequate experience or a lack of qualifications.
- ✔ **Hybrid or combination resume.** A blend of styles — a skill summary followed by a reverse chronological listing of your work experience. Hybrid resumes can work if you ensure you are marketing both your skills and a solid work history laid out in reverse date order.

Focusing on skills: The functional resume format

The functional format focuses on your skills and competencies rather than your work history. Functional resumes list all your relevant work experience and achievements under skill headings instead of individual job titles. You then include a bare-bones version of your work history at the end of your resume, listing job titles, employers and years.

 Pick out three or four skills to accentuate and present these as headings in order of importance, with the top skill listed first. Under the skill headings, include a few achievements that demonstrate how the skill was used. A functional resume is shown in Figure 2-2.

We go into more detail about listing your key skills in Chapter 3.

Functional Resume

Leanne Harvey
- Unit 2/77 Andrews Ave, Daw Park SA 5041   ■ m: 4444 444 444   ■ e: lharvey@email.com.au

Professional Qualifications

2012   **Certificate III in Community Pharmacy**   Pharmacy Guild of Australia

Relevant Skills & Experience

Retail
- Operated point of sale equipment, processed credit card transactions, used an EFTPOS machine and scanners.
- Cash handling and balanced the cash register at the end of the shift.
- Priced, ordered, coded and stored stock.
- Completed annual stocktakes.
- Designed window and in-store displays.

Customer service
- Provided advice and information to customers on products and services.
- Resolved and followed up on customer issues and complaints.
- Handled telephone enquiries and responded to customer requests promptly and professionally.

Sales
- Recognised as 'One of the Top 5 Salespeople of the Month' for three consecutive months.
- Increased sales by 10% through cross-selling and up-selling products to customers.
- Consistently exceeded monthly sales targets.

Work History

2012 – Present	Pharmacy Assistant	Mal's Discount Pharmacy, Marion
2010 – 2011	2IC	Gold Hill Jewellers, Marion
2008 – 2009	Sales Assistant	Gold Hill Jewellers, Marion

Computer Skills

MS Word (Advanced); MS Excel (Advanced); MS Access (Intermediate); MS PowerPoint (Advanced)

Referees available upon request

Figure 2-2: The functional resume highlights your skills rather than your work history.

The strengths of the functional resume are

- ✔ It downplays work history, whereas it highlights transferable skills you've acquired through all sorts of experiences (volunteer work, extracurricular activities, unpaid work experience), not just paid employment.

- ✔ You can choose skill headings that match the requirements of an advertised role. For example, if the job ad says a company requires someone with exceptional customer service skills, you can use 'Customer Service' as one of your headings.

- ✔ It hides employment gaps and periods of instability at first glance — hopefully long enough to get an employer interested.

The weaknesses of the functional resume are

- ✔ Employers can view functional formats with suspicion. By moving away from the traditional reverse chronological format, the recruiter may believe you're trying to hide something.

- ✔ Recruiters often find the functional format frustrating and difficult to follow. It doesn't outline exactly what you did in each of your jobs, and the recruiter or employer often has to second-guess which skills and achievements were acquired in which roles.

- ✔ Because the functional format presents your experience under skill headings, it fails to highlight career growth within an industry.

Mixing with the hybrids: The combination resume format

A hybrid resume — also called a combination resume — is a cross between the reverse chronological and functional formats. At the top of your resume is a list of your key skills or a summary of your skills, followed by a reverse chronological listing of your work history. You create a hybrid resume by grouping all your work experience into skill clusters (using the same format as in the functional resume) in the first section of your resume. This is followed by a list of your work experience laid out in reverse chronological order detailing dates of employment, job titles, company names, responsibilities and achievements. Figure 2-3 shows an example of a hybrid resume.

Combination Resume

SCOTT CAMPBELL
300 Punt Road, St Kilda VIC 3182
Ph: (03) 3333 3333 M: 0414 333 222
E: scampbell@email.com.au
Blog: www.planforlife.com.au

CAREER SUMMARY

Highly motivated Financial Planner with a proven track record of exceeding sales targets, client retention, identifying new business opportunities and building quality referral networks. Professional, confident, organised, adaptable and detail-oriented.

Areas of expertise:

- Pre & post retirement planning
- Insurance
- Superannuation
- Gearing
- Redundancy
- Wealth creation
- Estate planning
- Margin lending

EXPERIENCE & ACHIEVEMENTS

Customer Service

- Grew the client base from zero to 425 within an 18 month period.
- Received written commendations and gifts from clients for exceptional service and advice.

Financial Planning

- Awarded 'Top Consumer Planner in Australia' and ranked #2 Financial Planner across all business divisions in 2013
- Received 'Top Risk Revenue Planner' award 2012, 2013
- Recognised as the bank's 'Top Risk Writer' 2011

EMPLOYMENT HISTORY

Financial Planner

ABC Bank, August 2008 – Present

XYZ Bank, August 2006 – July 2008

1

Figure 2-3: A combination of both — the hybrid format (page 1 of 2).

SCOTT CAMPBELL

- Capitalise on new business opportunities and establish and develop relationships with centres of influence.
- Interview clients to gather information on their current financial position, goals and objectives.
- Prepare and present a strategic financial plan (statement of advice) tailored to client needs, outlining investment, superannuation and insurance options.
- Implement financial plan as agreed with client.
- Revisit client portfolios annually or as appropriate for the client.

Customer Service Representative

XYZ Bank, August 2003 – July 2006

- Answered inbound calls, identified customers' banking needs and referred business opportunities to relevant specialists.
- Handled customer enquiries regarding account balances, fees and charges, credit card limits, resetting passwords and paying bills through BPAY.
- Opened new accounts.
- Updated customer details.
- Kept customers informed of new products and services.
- Cross-selling and up-selling products to customers.
- Resolved customer issues and escalated complaints to the Team Leader.

EDUCATION

Graduate Diploma of Financial Planning,
Securities Institute of Australia, 2007

Bachelor of Business in Banking & Finance,
Victoria University, 2003

PROFESSIONAL MEMBERSHIPS

- Member, Australian Financial Advisers (AFA)
- Member, Financial Planning Association (FPA)

Referees available upon request

2

Figure 2-3: Continued (page 2 of 2).

A hybrid resume could be used if

- ✔ You want to match your skills to a particular job.

- ✔ You're a recent graduate wanting to highlight the skills you've acquired through extracurricular activities, volunteer work and paid employment.

- ✔ You've taken on lots of temporary jobs in the past.

- ✔ You've worked for one company for years, moving up the ranks and acquiring a diverse range of skills.

The pluses of using the hybrid format are

- ✔ Recruiters get an overview of your skills as well as your work history.

- ✔ Marketing your skills at the beginning of your resume diverts attention away from your work experience.

- ✔ Recruiters can still follow your employment timeline.

- ✔ Your transferable skills are highlighted.

The minuses of a combination resume are

- ✔ Some recruiters find them too 'fluffy'.

- ✔ Recruiters may not read through the whole resume after perusing the skills headings.

- ✔ Hybrid resumes can be lengthy, taking longer to read and write.

Targeting a Specific Job or Company

A targeted resume is personalised to a specific company or job. This type of resume aims to convince the employer that you're a perfect match for the job.

Putting in extra effort and tailoring your resume to a company or job immediately sets you apart from other applicants who churn out mass-produced documents. Targeted resumes stand out from the rest because they're unique and focused.

For more detail on all the resume elements that you can target for each employer, see Chapter 3.

Don't rush writing this kind of resume — put time and effort into researching the company. Make sure you have a clear understanding of the job before you start typing, and check to see you have what it takes to do the job — if you don't, don't apply.

Figure 2-4 shows you how to construct a targeted resume. For this example, Rebecca is applying for a role as an Administration Assistant/Receptionist — notice how the resume is closely aligned to the job.

The benefits of using a targeted resume include

- ✔ You make a good first impression. You demonstrate to the recruiter you've done your homework, you know the job well and have a genuine desire to work for the company.

- ✔ The employer can instantly see if you're the right fit for the job.

- ✔ You show the employer you know what you want to do — you're not applying for jobs willy-nilly.

The weaknesses of the targeted resume include

- ✔ An impractical format if you're applying for multiple jobs.

- ✔ Time consuming — you need a different resume for each job you apply for.

- ✔ Suits only one position — employers may not consider you for other vacancies.

Targeted Resume

Rebecca Hawkins

Unit 5/66 Collins Street, New Farm QLD 4005
m: 1111 111 111
e: rhawkins@email.com.au

Career Profile

Accomplished PA with extensive expertise in reception and office administration, I also have experience working in a small office environment. Highly organised with excellent time management skills, I work well under pressure, managing multiple tasks and priorities to meet deadlines.

Key Skills

- Articulate communicator with a warm and professional telephone manner.
- Well developed interpersonal skills with a proven ability to build relationships with clients, suppliers and managers.
- Capable of working independently or as part of a team.
- Enthusiastic, confident, efficient, accurate and detail focused.
- Typing speed of 70 wpm with 99% accuracy.
- Computer literate with advanced proficiency in MS Word, Excel, PowerPoint and Access, and intermediate proficiency with MYOB accounting software.

WORK EXPERIENCE

Personal Assistant
August 2010 – Present

McFadden & Associates Pty Ltd

Responsibilities:

- Provide administration and office support to four accountants.
- Schedule weekly team meetings, prepare agendas, generate and distribute MYOB reports to all staff.
- Interact with banking institutions, the Australian Taxation Office (ATO) and the Australian Securities and Investments Commission (ASIC).
- Code bank statements using BankLink.
- Collate income tax returns and financial statements.
- Follow up with clients on missing or outstanding information.
- Advise clients by telephone of tax return completion.
- Lodge documents with the Australian Taxation Office and the Australian Securities and Investments Commission.
- Prepare reports, PowerPoint presentations and other routine correspondence.
- General admin, including typing invoices and undertaking the payment of accounts, opening and processing mail, and faxing, photocopying, binding and scanning of documents.

Achievements:

- Grew the client base by 25% through initiating direct mail campaigns to new and existing businesses in the area.

Figure 2-4: Targeted resumes are aimed at a specific company or job (page 1 of 2).

2

Rebecca Hawkins
_____

(Work experience continued)

Overseas travel
(November 2009 – June 2010)

Receptionist/Personal Assistant
(February 2006 – October 2009)
Goss Chartered Accountants
Responsibilities:
- Welcomed clients and visitors to the office.
- Managed the front office reception and operated a busy switchboard (8 lines).
- Answered the telephone, screened calls, handled enquiries and forwarded messages to the appropriate staff member.
- Managed the partner's diary, scheduled client appointments, organised conferences and coordinated travel and accommodation requirements.
- Advised clients of the documentation required to set up a new company.
- Liaised with clients, the Australian Taxation Office (ATO), Australian Securities and Investments Commission (ASIC) and other government agencies.
- Updated client records on the database.
- Filed confidential correspondence for the partners and maintained an efficient records management system.
- Trained and supervised three junior clerical staff.
- Word processed partner's dictation tapes, typed minutes of meetings, and prepared routine correspondence.
- Planned and coordinated client seminars with responsibility for sending invitations, booking conference rooms, organising catering, preparing name tags and creating PowerPoint presentations.
- Ordered stationery supplies and maintained office equipment, furniture and fittings.

Achievements

- Reduced stationery expenses by 10% through ordering office supplies online.
- Received the Outstanding Staff Member of the Year Award in 2008.

EDUCATION

Diploma of the Institute of Professional Secretaries and Administrators

Deakin University

completed in 2006

PROFESSIONAL DEVELOPMENT

Create and use databases (Access 1 — BSBADM 305A)

Southbank Institute of Technology completed in 2010.

REFEREES

Available on request

Figure 2-4: Continued (page 2 of 2).

The targeted format is suitable if

- ✓ You know the job inside and out.
- ✓ You're responding to a specific job ad or vacancy.
- ✓ You want to tailor your resume to a particular company.
- ✓ You're applying internally for jobs in your current organisation.

This format is not suitable if

- ✓ You don't have a lot of time.
- ✓ Research is not your forte.

Compiling a Curriculum Vitae: The CV

You often hear the terms resume and curriculum vitae (usually called a CV) used interchangeably these days. Nine times out of ten, when a person is talking about a CV he or she is generally referring to your resume, but a CV is a little different to a resume.

Used mainly by professionals in highly academic fields that generally require long years of study, a CV is longer: Page length for a CV can be up to ten pages or more, depending on your level of experience. A resume is much briefer because you're highlighting your skills, qualifications, attributes and professional experience — a bit like a sales brochure advertising your strengths to a potential employer. A CV is far more comprehensive and information-based and details your awards, honours, fellowships, publications, presentations, conferences, community projects and research work. CVs can be long-winded and dull to read — a good cure for insomnia!

You come across CVs in the medical, research, academic, teaching or scientific professions. A CV gives the recruiter an overview of your professional and academic accomplishments. You show the recruiter how competent you are in your field of work.

A CV is a good choice for doctors, researchers, teachers, scientists, clinicians, academics and other professionals who work in a PhD environment. Unless the position especially requests a CV, stick to using a conventional resume.

Handy hints for CV headings

No one set way exists to prepare a CV, but here are some pointers to help you create a winning format. Remember to update your CV regularly, and adapt it for each job — only include information that is relevant to the role.

✔ Make sure your CV is clearly laid out and easy to follow. Keep the information well organised and don't get too complicated.

✔ Put the most important information at the top.

✔ Be consistent with your formatting — a simple layout works best.

✔ Avoid padding your CV with unnecessary details or repeating information.

Headings commonly used in a CV:

✔ Contact details

✔ Qualifications — postgraduate and undergraduate qualifications

✔ Masters thesis or project

✔ Awards/honours/scholarships

✔ Registration/licences/certifications

✔ Professional experience

✔ Fieldwork

✔ Research experience

✔ Consulting experience

✔ Volunteer work or community involvement

✔ Technical skills

✔ Workshops/conferences attended

✔ Publications

✔ Presentations

✔ Grants received

✔ Fellowships

✔ Patents

✔ Professional memberships, advisory boards and committees

✔ International travel/overseas study

✔ Languages

✔ Referees

Part II
Designing a Dazzling Resume

Common Section Headings Used in Resumes

Contact details	Awards and honours	Holiday work/internship
Career objective	Work experience	Additional skills
Career goal	Experience	Technical skills
Career summary	Employment	Computer skills
Summary	Employment history	Software
Profile	Work history	IT skills
Professional profile	Part-time work	Extracurricular activities
Career statement	Professional experience	Languages
Capability statement	Projects	Licences/registrations
Career highlights	Other experience	Training courses
Achievements	Skills	Professional development
Education	Key skills	Professional memberships
Courses	Skills summary	Memberships
Education and training	Skills and expertise	Memberships and associations
Professional qualifications	Professional skills	Interests
Qualifications	Voluntary experience	Interests and activities
Certifications	Community involvement	Activities
Accomplishments	University/community involvement	Referees

web extras

Visit www.dummies.com/extras/writingresumes coverlettersau for free tips and tricks for designing a dazzling resume.

In this part . . .

✔ Create the perfect mix of content for your resume, from the essential ingredients to the optional flavours.

✔ Spice up your resume with powerful action verbs, and use keywords to make sure you stand out from the crowd (and in an online database!).

✔ Employ some practical advice and simple strategies to help overcome those tricky resume dilemmas.

✔ Check over your resume and make those last-minute finishing touches before you send it off to the recruiter.

Chapter 3

Creating the Contents

· ·

In This Chapter

▶ Getting acquainted with the parts of a resume

▶ Making your resume reflect who you are

▶ Piecing the parts together

· ·

*T*hink of writing resumes as like baking a cake. For the cake, you need a recipe to guide you and a good mix of the right ingredients to ensure you create something that is easy for recruiters and employers to digest. Resume writing is exactly the same. You need to follow a resume recipe: Blend together a combination of skills, experience, qualifications and achievements, then top it all off with an icing of marketing and individuality.

The trick to developing a great resume is to create content with substance. A well-structured resume engages the reader and presents your work history in a logical and sequential order. A recruiter needs to gain a good understanding of where you worked, for how long, what was happening in each of your roles, and what skills, knowledge and experience you acquired along the way.

In this chapter, we introduce you to the main parts of a resume, from the seemingly simple task of listing your name and contact details to whether or not to list referees. Get these elements right and you're well on your way to tasting employment success.

Cooking Up a Winning Resume

Your resume should be easy to read at speed and contain lots of great information demonstrating why you are qualified for the role you are applying for. A recruitment consultant or employer should be able to run their eye down the length of your career history without seeing any unexplained gaps. Whether you took four years off to raise your child or four months off to travel the country, make sure you explain this information in a line or two in your career history.

So, how do you go about whipping up a resume that rises to the occasion and cooks up interviews for you? Resume writing is a piece of cake once you get started. Here are the essential ingredients you need to include to attract the instant interest of an employer:

- ✔ Contact information
- ✔ Work experience and achievements
- ✔ Education
- ✔ Referees

Here are some optional ingredients that you can include to add flavour to your resume:

- ✔ Career objective
- ✔ Career profile (sometimes known as a career summary)
- ✔ Key skills
- ✔ IT skills, including social media skills
- ✔ Languages (if relevant to the job)
- ✔ Professional memberships
- ✔ Hobbies and interests (if relevant to the job)

Writing a resume takes time, effort and energy. Don't destroy your chances by taking short cuts. You will not be there when your resume is read, so you won't be able to explain how that careless spelling mistake is not a reflection of your work ethic, or that the unexplained six-month gap in your career history was actually spent caring for a sick parent. The fact you are reading this book means you are prepared to do what it takes to make your resume perfect — so congratulations on your winning attitude!

Whatever you do, remember your resume needs to measure up to expectations and should contain the essential information.

The sole purpose of your resume is to provide recruiters with information about you — who you are, what skills you have, and how you can add value to an organisation. By *adding value*, we mean how you can take the job, make it your own and add that something extra. In the following sections we cover the intricacies of creating a successful resume, so let's start at the top, with the essential ingredients.

Confirming your contact details

Recruiters and employers need to be able to access your contact details quickly and easily, especially if you're shortlisted for an interview. Place your contact information at the top of your resume, either aligned to the left of the page or centred to make it stand out. Here's the information you start with, preferably in this order:

- ✔ **Name:** Use the name you prefer to be addressed by at work. Use a slightly larger font and a bold typeface to capture attention.

  If people usually find your name hard to pronounce, write the phonetic pronunciation in brackets. Some overseas-born candidates choose a local-sounding name and place their birth name in brackets or vice versa. This is totally up to you. For example, if your Chinese name is Xiong Wang but you go by the first name Danny, write Xiong (Danny) Wang or Danny (Xiong) Wang on your resume. You can opt for only including your local name (Danny Wang), but remember that once you are employed, you will need to use your official name on employment forms.

- ✔ **Mailing address:** List a current address with the street name, suburb, state and postcode. You could also choose to only list your name, phone and email details on your resume: Some employers will have no issue with this and others will.

  Many recruiters will only consider 'local' job applicants, so demonstrate this by including your address. On the other hand, there is such a thing as 'postcode' prejudice (where a candidate lives far away from the job's location, creating concerns around reliability and punctuality). If you are worried about this, include these qualities in your list of key skills (see the section 'Including a list of key skills', later in this chapter, for more on your key skills list).

Some candidates may be transient, such as students and members of the armed forces, in which case an email may prove a better contact point.

✔ **Telephone numbers and mobiles:** List home or mobile phone numbers where you can readily answer the phone or where the employer can leave a message. Always include the area code followed by the number. If you list your home phone number, make sure you divert your phone to an answering machine or a voicemail service. Review your voicemail message and even re-record it to ensure you speak slowly, clearly and sound as professional as possible. And if you have family members at home during the day answering calls, make sure they conduct themselves appropriately and can take messages.

Beware of using fancy jingles or answering machine messages that are humorous. You may think being greeted by the *Mission Impossible* theme is entertaining, but to a recruiter this may seem unprofessional. Remember, your mission, if you choose to accept it, is to create a favourable impression.

You can list your work number, particularly if you have a direct line and voicemail facilities, but if you would rather only receive calls via your mobile phone state that in a note with your application. By using your mobile, you can keep it on silent during work time and check messages in your breaks and then choose a quiet, private space before returning a recruiter's call.

✔ **Email address:** Email is an important point of contact: It is easy for recruiters and employers to use and you can review your messages from wherever you are via a hand-held device.

Ensure your email address includes your name rather than a funky handle like queenbee@xyz.com.au. Your resume is marketing you as an outstanding employee so every piece of information must support your goal of getting the job.

✔ **URL:** If you have a work-related blog or you are a designer and have a web page showcasing your work, include the URL in your resume. Include this detail just below your contact details at the top of your resume.

✔ **Citizenship:** If you're not from Australia or New Zealand, state that you have a work permit or citizenship. Again, this detail is best placed just below your contact details so an employer or recruiter can tell you're eligible to work at just a quick glance.

What's in a name?

When your name is unique or unusual, providing the phonetic pronunciation in brackets will assist the recruiter or employer when they want to contact you. Research carried out in Australia suggests that resumes from people with exotic-sounding names get over-looked in favour of those with Anglo Saxon-sounding names. Is this racism or something else?

Prejudice can lurk anywhere, even in the minds of recruiters and hiring managers. However, the rise of the Internet could be another reason why resumes with 'foreign-sounding' names do not progress into the short-list pile. While a recruitment agency may promote itself as being based in Australia or New Zealand, the World Wide Web is global, so job listings can attract applications from all corners of the planet, including candidates with no right to work in the country where the job is based. Recruiters and employers want to fill a job with a qualified candidate who is ready to go — and preferably with local knowl-edge — as soon as possible: This explains why time-poor recruiters ignore resumes they suspect are from overseas candidates. Play up your ties to Australia and New Zealand by including your birth country or the years you have resided in this neck of the woods.

Don't list your date of birth, marital status, gender, age or religion in your personal details. This information is irrelevant, and it's unlawful for you to be selected or eliminated on the basis of these factors. Don't tempt employers or recruiters into making a judgement about anything but your skills and qualifications.

Photos, fancy cover pages or other distracting extras will not win you any points and could get your application binned.

Recording your work experience

When documenting your work experience, always list your most recent job first and go back in reverse chronological order. For jobs you want to emphasise, list the following:

- Job title
- Company name
- Dates of employment (months and years)

- Company description if organisation is not well known
- Responsibilities
- Achievements

For jobs you don't want to emphasise, only list

- Job title
- Company name and location
- Dates of employment (months and years)

If you're a high-flyer who's climbed the career ladder or worked for prestigious companies, highlight this by including a brief overview of your employment history on the front page of your resume, listing positions, companies and dates under a heading

Explaining overseas experience

Employers in Australia and New Zealand are sometimes viewed as parochial — Australia in particular. They want people who have 'local knowledge'; but what they really want is someone who can get up to speed quickly and start delivering the goods.

Candidates from overseas can help the employer or recruiter understand the value of their experience by putting it in a local context. Here are some example scenarios that highlight just how easily you can miss an opportunity to sell your expertise:

- You can't rely on a recruiter or employer understanding that a particular Italian company is the largest department store in the country with one of the most advanced merchandising systems in Europe — experience that could benefit you when applying for a merchandising role in a department store in Auckland or Brisbane.

- An IT project manager from India worked on the roll-out of a new computer system for a major teaching hospital. However, when he listed the job role he neglected to explain that the employer was a hospital, or that the computer system was the most advanced of its kind in the region.

You can also compare a place you worked overseas with a local company. For example, the *South China Morning Post* newspaper and website is the leading English-language daily in Hong Kong, not unlike the *Sydney Morning Herald*.

This sort of detail helps the recruiter imagine you filling the role on offer, and will increase your chances of being shortlisted for a job interview.

such as 'Career Overview' or 'Employment Summary'. This can be very handy for recruiters, who like to go straight to your work experience to check out your background.

Outlining your responsibilities

Responsibilities are the things you're paid to do in a job. *Achievements* demonstrate the way you have added value in a job — but more on that in the next section.

It is tempting to list every little thing you do in your current role to prove your suitability for your next job; however, this approach won't help you and will just take up valuable real estate on your resume that could be better used for selling your unique skills.

Each responsibility statement should commence with an action verb, followed by a description of the task. Action verbs usually end in 'ed' and describe how you performed the task or action. Here are some examples of job responsibilities with action verbs:

- ✔ **Facilitated** [action verb] weekly induction training and conducted [action verb] orientation tours for new staff [description of the task]

- ✔ **Typed** [action verb] court documentation including interrogatories, subpoenas, affidavits, offers to settle, plaints and writs [description of the task]

- ✔ **Logged** [action verb] help desk calls and provided hardware and software support to customers [description of the task]

See Chapter 4 for some more examples of action verbs you can use when writing your resume.

When you compile your responsibilities, use past tense for previous experience and present tense for current roles. See how the action verbs change using different tenses.

> Previous role: **Facilitated** weekly induction training [past tense]
>
> Current role: **Facilitate** weekly induction training [present tense]

Consider the following statement:

> Liaised with external clients

Notice how vague the statement is. This statement doesn't tell the reader how you liaised with the clients. Was it by phone, in person or through correspondence? What were you liaising with the clients about? Your resume needs to include specific responsibilities. Try this instead:

> Dealt with clients on the phone, listened to their legal requests and redirected the calls to the appropriate solicitor.

When writing your responsibilities, you need to take a step back and think about what you actually do or did in your role. What were your responsibilities? What were you accountable for? Write your tasks down succinctly and try not to waffle. A recruiter wants a crystal clear understanding of your career to date.

Extolling your achievements

In recruitment there is a saying, 'the greatest predictor of future behaviour is past behaviour'. Listing at least three to four achievements for each of your past two to three roles is a good way to show off the sort of pizzazz and 'can-do' attitude you'll bring to your next role. An *achievement* demonstrates how you went above and beyond the call of duty to really put your mark on the role.

Writing achievements can be a wee bit daunting when you first start off. Try to look at it from the employer's point of view and see the inclusion of achievements as assisting the decision-making process. The best achievements are those that lead to measurable success or improvements. If a process you introduced saved time, include by how much and any cost savings that resulted from your actions. A salesperson is paid to hit 100 per cent of target, so listing that you consistently hit 110 per cent of target for four months is a quantifiable achievement. Detail specifically the action you took and the result.

Here are some sample achievements to modify for your own resume:

- Designed a file-tracking system [achievement] that increased efficiency and reduced the time spent locating missing documents by up to 30 minutes per search [benefit].

- Decreased staff turnover by 35 per cent [benefit] through developing company-wide incentive programs, employee satisfaction surveys and in-house training [achievement].

✔ Initiated and developed a payroll procedures manual [achievement], which improved accuracy and reduced processing errors by 50 per cent [benefit].

✔ Grew the customer base from zero to 500 within two years [benefit], by cold-calling customers and launching a direct mail campaign to new and existing businesses in the area [achievement].

In some circumstances, listing a benefit for every achievement isn't practical. In these cases, just specify the achievement. For example:

Won 'Telesales Award' for excellence in customer service.

If you're a manager (or a high-flying executive), be specific about what you've been doing in each role. For example, if you're managing a project, include information about the type of project, size, achievements and key milestones.

Showing off your schooling, education and training

Document your most recent qualifications first. Put any postgraduate studies you've completed before your undergraduate qualifications. Feature high-school details only if you've recently graduated from secondary school or uni — these details aren't necessary if you've studied years ago. Here's an example of how to present your high school qualifications:

South Australian Certificate of Education

Modbury High School, Adelaide (2007)

Make sure you list your university degrees before your certificate and diploma qualifications, and promote your formal qualifications before any short courses or seminars you have attended. Spell out the name of the qualification in full, listing the major, the institution that awarded the qualification and the year completed:

Bachelor of Science (Major in Computer Science)

University of Tasmania (2004)

Certificate IV in Information Technology

TAFE Tasmania (2000)

If you're in the middle of completing a qualification, list the same details in your resume, replacing the year with your expected completion date. For example:

Bachelor of Science (Major in Computer Science)

University of Tasmania (expected year of completion 2015)

If you're a graduate or school leaver, showcase any outstanding academic achievements. This is your chance to gain an edge over other job seekers, so don't be shy. List any prizes, awards or scholarships, and impress the recruiter with your high grade point average or university entrance score. Recruiters love top performers!

On the other hand, if you're a seasoned socialiser who's spent ten years completing a four-year bachelor degree and have a poor track record, you need to camouflage your results and supply them only upon request. And if you completed your degree decades ago, you're better off omitting the results. We provide more information for graduates in Chapter 12 and school leavers in Chapter 11.

Highlight professional development or training courses you've attended but only if they relate to the job you're applying for. Completion of a software certification course, work skill course such as time management or people management and industry-based courses are all good examples of what to include. Take care when considering whether to include extracurricular courses. An Indonesian language course could be relevant to a role that includes travel to that country, but cake decorating could be left off. List the title of the course followed by where and when it was completed, similar to the example shown in Figure 3-1.

SALES POSITION:
Professional Development

Winning and Closing the Sale	Sales Training Australia	2011
Building Client Relationships	Sales Training Australia	2010
Sales Team Management	College of Sales & Marketing	2009

Figure 3-1: Listing relevant training courses.

If you have no higher education qualifications, impress the recruiter by drawing attention to the fact you've attended plenty of training courses, seminars, workshops and industry conferences relevant to the job you're applying for.

Recording relevant referees

No matter how skilled you are, referees can make or break your chances at the final hurdle. Due to the time and expense involved with reference checking, a company will often leave this part of the selection process until just before a job offer is made. Recruitment firms, particularly those recruiting contractors or employees for temporary assignments, may carry out reference checking early in the process. Here are some tips to follow when considering your list of referees:

- ✔ **Provide work-related referees:** Recruiters and employers usually want to speak to at least two people you reported to directly. The referee will be asked to verify the claims made in your resume and describe not just the job you did but also how you went about it. Written references and personal referees are not given much credibility these days and may not be accepted at all.

- ✔ **Choose your referees wisely:** Heard the tale of Dr Jekyll and Mr Hyde? Be cautious of who you nominate as a referee. Referees can ruin your job chances in one fell swoop. If you had a personality clash with your immediate supervisor, were sacked or forced to resign, your best alternative is to list a work colleague or another manager from the same organisation. Be prepared to justify your reasons to a recruiter for not including your immediate supervisor's name on the list. Sometimes you may need to eat humble pie and be honest. Ensure your other referees are strong and have supervised you in the past. Immersing the recruiter in a sea of favourable referees may be the life jacket you need to stay afloat.

- ✔ **Notify your referees in advance:** Excuse us while we climb on our soapbox. We can't stress enough how important it is to request permission before you use a referee. If you don't, be warned that some referees may react to your discourtesy by jeopardising your prospects in return. Believe us, we have completed truckloads of referee checks and interviewed plenty of reference checkers. Update your referees, particularly if you're actively searching for jobs and attending interviews.

✔ **List your current or past supervisor/s:** Don't feel pressured to list your current supervisor; however, make sure your other referees can comment on your work performance and have managed or worked with you in the past. You may even consider the option of listing your current supervisor as a referee, indicating on your resume in bold text that you would like to be contacted prior to your referee being phoned, allowing you time to prepare your boss for the unexpected.

Sometimes, listing a supervisor may be difficult or near impossible — particularly if you've managed or operated your own business. Perhaps you could nominate a customer, supplier or contractor as a referee, or anyone else who has built a constructive working relationship with you over the duration of your business.

If you're working for a company that prohibits giving verbal references over the phone, for fear of being sued, you can either ask for a written letter of reference or list a manager or a work colleague who may be prepared to act as a character referee.

✔ **Record referee details:** Provide the name of the referee, their title, company, phone number and, if practicable, an email address. If your referee has moved on and is working for a different organisation, list their current organisation and title, followed by a note in brackets substantiating the relationship.

The following is an example of how to present your referees:

Michael Smith

State Manager

KPT Enterprises (former direct supervisor at Yippie Beans Pty Ltd)

(07) 1111 1111 (w) michael.smith@kpt.com.au

Another approach you can use on your resume is to not disclose referee details but supply them on request. Type the words **Referees available on request** on your resume. This is a simple and easy alternative if you're struggling to locate the information, or you need time to track down your referees. Don't forget: After you have been for an interview the recruiter may contact you and need these details urgently.

Government jobs are an exception. When applying for government jobs you will need to list referee details in your written application. In this case, you have no option but to comply. As a general guide, include two or three referees in public sector applications.

Using the web to help tailor your resume

Researching a company is a must before you attend a job interview but it can also help you tailor your resume to ensure you come across as the kind of person they are looking for.

Visiting an employer's website is a good start, allowing you to check out the values and key priorities of the company. However, many companies also have a Facebook page and LinkedIn profile that can tell you a lot about the organisation. Facebook profiles usually include interaction with customers, providing new insight you will not see on a company website.

Company websites and their related social media activities often include job listings too, providing you with new job leads.

See Chapter 8 for more on how you can use social media to enhance your career opportunities.

Adding the Flavour: The Essence of You

After you've gathered the essential parts of your resume, you need to think about spicing up your resume with a few optional extras. Blow your own trumpet here, but be careful how you use these parts and remember to only include elements that relate specifically to the role you're applying for.

Selling your skills and experience up-front

The human eye scans a resume in less than 30 seconds — at least for the first time. A recruiter or employer may receive hundreds of applications for any single job at any one time.

They will also be working on a range of other projects in addition to recruiting for the role you have applied for. Recruitment firms and many large employers even use software programs to scan resumes for the first time. All this means either a time-poor human or a computer will be reading your resume.

The secret to writing a standout resume is to communicate quickly to a recruiter that you have what it takes to do the job. One way to create that favourable first impression is to provide a snapshot of yourself at the beginning of your resume to set a positive tone and engage the reader from the start. This can be a short paragraph introducing yourself, or a few succinct bullet points drawing attention to your skills, abilities, qualifications and experience. Give your summary one of the following titles: 'Summary', 'Career Profile', 'Career Summary', 'Professional Summary', 'Professional Profile', 'Highlights of Skills and Experience' — whatever title takes your fancy. Your career summary can include

- ✔ **Achievements:** Individual accomplishments or successes.

- ✔ **Experience:** Involvement in the career field.

- ✔ **Personal attributes:** Characteristics or individual qualities, such as loyalty, commitment, reliability, sense of humour, motivation, confidence, enthusiasm and professionalism.

- ✔ **Qualifications:** Relevant education, study or training in the area.

- ✔ **Skills:** Demonstrated ability to carry out or perform a specific task. Proficiency gained through work experience, training and study. Skills include technical, personal and transferable skills.

- ✔ **Competencies:** Skills and knowledge required to perform a job or job function to an acceptable standard.

- ✔ **Strengths:** Areas you excel in — your strong points.

If you find you're struggling to put your skills, strengths and personal attributes on paper, seek inspiration from a work colleague or manager. They see how you operate at work on a regular basis and can point out some strong points you never thought you had.

Pulling together your career profile doesn't need to be a chore. Just follow these steps:

1. **Look at the job ad or a copy of the job description and make a list of all the skills, competencies, personal attributes, experience and qualifications required to do the job.**

2. **Place a tick beside the skills and attributes you have (never lie and pretend you have skills you don't).**

3. **Create a bullet list, adding any strengths and personal attributes you have.**

4. **Incorporate the ticked and extra items into a summary of yourself in your resume.**

Look at the following list and note the key skills (in bold) for a number of different professions:

- ✔ Known for being **organised**, **efficient**, **flexible** and **confidential** (personal assistant role)

- ✔ **Analytical**, **accurate** and **methodical** with strong **attention to detail** (accountant role)

- ✔ Top sales representative with a proven track record of **exceeding targets**, **winning sales** and **generating new and repeat business** (sales rep role)

- ✔ Well-developed **communication skills**, with a **cheerful disposition** and a **professional telephone manner** (call centre operator)

- ✔ **Competent**, **self-motivated** designer with **creative flair** and a **can-do attitude** (graphic design role)

Notice how the strengths listed in bold correlate well with the key attributes and skills you would expect of someone in that industry or role.

We look at career summaries, career objectives and key skills lists in more detail in the next section.

A cover letter also demonstrates how your skills and experience match the job. We provide advice on how to create the perfect cover letter in Chapter 7.

Career profile versus career objective: What's right for you?

Simply put, a career profile (sometimes also called a career summary) shows an employer what you are going to do for them, while a career objective tells the employer what you want them to do for you.

For this reason, a career profile is better suited to those with an established career or work history, and a career objective is more helpful for school leavers, and TAFE and university graduates. You can read more about resumes for school leavers in Chapter 11 and resumes for graduates in Chapter 12.

As an example, we're going to take a junior marketing professional going for a job in a digital agency, and create a career profile only and then in a separate example, add in a career objective:

> Career Profile
>
> A marketing coordinator with two years' experience in a digital agency, I hold a Bachelor of Marketing degree and have completed several specialist courses on topics including social media and Google analytics. With excellent time management skills and a keen eye for detail, I am also proficient in the full suite of Microsoft Office as well as several other relevant programs.

Always use short, concise sentences that focus on a particular skill you have or specific area of experience that relates to the job. Your career profile should capture the recruiter's or employer's attention quickly, as well as demonstrate why you are a relevant candidate for the job on offer. For younger candidates, including a career objective as the last sentence in your career profile can also help recruiters and employers remember you as they sift through big piles of applicants. Remember to align your objective to what the employer is looking for in a new hire — namely, someone interested in what his or her business is trying to achieve.

We will use the same candidate in the following example, keeping in mind that the digital agency the candidate is hoping to join in this example specialises in the retail sector.

> Career Profile
>
> A marketing coordinator with two years' experience in a digital agency, I hold a Bachelor of Marketing degree and have completed several specialist courses on

topics including social media and Google analytics. With excellent time management skills and a keen eye for detail, I am also proficient in the full suite of Microsoft Office as well as several other relevant programs. My career objective in the near future is to further develop my skills in creating measurable and successful online campaigns for the retail sector.

In this example, the candidate has aligned their career ambitions to what the hiring company does. This helps the employer imagine you in the role being advertised, and also positions you as possible promotion material.

The career profile heading can be centred to make it stand out.

Me, myself and I: Using personal pronouns

Until recently, it was accepted wisdom that personal pronouns such as 'I', 'my' and 'me' should be avoided at all costs when writing a resume, and that a more traditional approach (writing in the third person) was the only way to go. These days, with the proliferation of social media and the ease of modern communication, it's perfectly acceptable to bring out the 'I's and 'my's to give your resume a more personal, direct feel.

Using personal pronouns in your career profile or career objective works particularly well to help you talk directly to the recruiter or employer, injecting professional passion into your career aspirations. However, it makes sense not to overuse personal pronouns: Try to keep them to a minimum outside of these sections.

Social media platforms such as LinkedIn, Facebook and Twitter have no doubt encouraged this more flexible attitude to professional language, so utilise these platforms to present a well-rounded personal 'brand' and let your resume complement your online presence. For more on social media, and how you can use it to support your career development, see Chapter 8.

Remember, however, that sometimes writing in the third person is still the most appropriate course of action. Some employers and recruiters prefer candidates to take a more traditional approach, particularly senior executives. Therefore, know your audience and tailor your resume accordingly. For example, your choice of language when creating an application for Google will be different to that used in an application for a local accountancy firm.

For more on choosing the right words for your resume, see Chapter 4.

Relevancy is the name of the game with a resume. Think of your resume as valuable real estate. Don't take up your valuable real estate with anything that does not serve a purpose. All information must add to the story of you being the best person for the job.

Sharing your career objective

A career objective is a succinct statement of your career intentions that provides a recruiter with valuable insight into your aspirations, motivations and achievement drive.

Here are some useful points to think about before stating your career objective:

- ✔ Limit your career objective to a few sentences. Keep it simple.

- ✔ Target it to the job you're applying for.

- ✔ Keep it realistic, achievable and measurable. An entry-level graduate aspiring to move up the ladder to managing director of a big multinational company in 12 months may be a teensy-weensy bit ambitious and unrealistic.

- ✔ Draw attention to the skills and experience you have acquired. Focus on what you can do for the employer.

- ✔ Ensure your career objective is not so broad or general that it becomes a meaningless filler.

- ✔ Avoid writing career objectives that are too narrow — this may limit your job prospects within an organisation. Mentioning a specific title such as marketing officer or human resource assistant may pigeonhole you and limit your exposure to other jobs in the same or similar field.

Career objectives can be particularly useful when you've recently graduated or have a diverse career background, and when you're changing careers or re-entering the workforce and want to convey to the recruiter your career intentions. Here are some examples of career objectives:

- ✔ **Accounting**: An entry-level position in a top-tier professional services firm with opportunities to apply my accounting knowledge and business skills in a commercial environment. Interest in audit. Long-term plans to achieve partnership.

- ✔ **Administration**: To secure a junior office role in the medical industry where I can utilise my skills in administration, reception and customer service.

When developing a career objective, avoid using descriptions that say nothing such as 'my career objective is to utilise my skills in a professional way for the benefit of myself and my employer'. Not only is that what every employee is paid to do, but it also offers the potential employer no greater understanding of you. Be specific about your goals and tailor your career objective to the job you are going for.

Keep your career objectives short and succinct — avoid long-winded explanations.

Including a list of key skills

A list of your key skills is presented as bullet points near the top of your resume. You don't necessarily need a career profile and a list of key skills, but you can have both if this provides you with an advantage.

A list of key skills can boost your chances

- ✔ **When a job requires a number of technical skills.** By placing these in a list at near the top of your resume, you establish that you meet the 'must have' skills for the role.

- ✔ **When a recruiter is using the Internet to locate the right person for the job.** Using a list of key skills boosts the chances of your resume popping up in the right search results.

To decide which key skills to include in your list, view the advertisement or job description for the role you're going for and underline all the words used to describe the employer's criteria for the role. Now, compare this list with your own skills and qualifications. By completing this simple exercise, you're ready to write your list.

Some examples of suitable key skills for different professions include

- ✔ **IT programmer:** Programming languages they are proficient in

- ✔ **Journalist:** Working to very short deadlines, reporting on areas of expertise

- ✔ **Tradesperson:** Any certifications required

To prepare the following example, we looked at a real job ad for a claims consultant in a Christchurch insurance firm. Your key skills list for this job might include

- ✔ Experience handling earthquake-related claims
- ✔ Three years' experience in commercial insurance and two years' experience in domestic insurance
- ✔ Excellent time management skills
- ✔ Proven record as a proactive problem solver
- ✔ Staff award winner for teamwork

See Chapter 4 for some examples of key skills lists in action.

Mentioning memberships

Including memberships in professional or industry-based associations can further demonstrate your commitment and interest in your chosen career. The recruiter or employer may even be a member of the same association, creating a shared point of interest, so be sure to only include genuine details.

Also include any special responsibilities you may hold with the association, such as being an office bearer or member of a committee or group.

Including hobbies and interests

Recruitment consultants and HR professionals welcome hobbies and interests because it helps them make small talk with candidates who are then interviewed. It also brings the work person to life in a larger way beyond their work skills. However, on the flip side, a hobby could just as easily become a source of prejudice or concern. We certainly don't think that's fair, but we know it can be a reality. For example, a recruiter shared a story with us involving an employer who was starting a new IT company. He favoured a candidate who had listed extreme sports as a hobby because he wanted 'risk-takers' and ignored a highly skilled candidate who had listed guitar playing as a hobby. Listing memberships in political, religious or activist groups is also best avoided.

When listing interests and hobbies in your resume, always keep the following tips in mind:

✔ Never lie about your hobbies and interests. The recruiter may bring up the topic in the interview, particularly if they have a special interest in the activity.

✔ Include personal interests that demonstrate your transferable skills and personal attributes. For example, listing karate on your resume shows the recruiter you're self-disciplined and focused, whereas playing chess reveals you are tactical and strategic.

✔ Jot down any job-related interests. Saying you invest in your spare time adds value to a financial planner's resume. Mentioning that you renovate houses on weekends looks good if you're going for a job in real estate.

✔ Don't put in controversial activities that may send the wrong message to recruiters. Similarly, avoid mentioning outside interests and hobbies that may raise concerns about your commitment to the job (such as running your own small business on the side).

✔ If you're a graduate with limited work experience, beef up your resume with interests and extracurricular activities that demonstrate your leadership ability, communication and interpersonal skills, teamwork and community involvement.

✔ Find out if the company you're applying to sponsors golf days, triathlons, touch football competitions or other corporate sporting events. If you enjoy playing the sport, list it in your resume. This establishes common ground with the recruiter and shows you'll fit the corporate culture.

Listing boards, committees and taskforces

If you're an executive, don't forget to mention in your resume the fact that you've sat on boards, chaired a committee, served on a taskforce or taken on a voluntary leadership role in a not-for-profit or professional association. For example:

Member, Quality Task Force, 2013

Chairman, Water Conservation Committee, 2013

Board member, Business Council of Australia, 2013

Non-Executive Director, Woolworths, 2013

President, Dandenong Cricket Club, 2013

Council member, National Gallery of Australia, 2013

Showcasing your awards

Include any awards for outstanding achievement and excellence in your resume.

Being seen as the expert

If you've written a column for a leading website, articles for an industry magazine, got your work published in a book or have public speaking experience, impress the recruiter by including these details in your resume. This will boost your credibility and you'll be perceived as an 'expert' in your field. Here are some examples to illustrate how you'd show this in your resume:

Guest speaker, Executive Business Luncheon, NSW

Business Chamber, 2013

Keynote presenter, CPA Congress, 2012

Putting It All Together

With only 30 seconds of a recruiter's time to create a powerful impression, you need to maximise this opportunity and develop a resume that's tailored to the job and generates interviews. Generally, employers decide after reading the first couple of pages of your resume whether they want to interview you. You only have one opportunity, so make an impact.

Think carefully about the role you're applying for and adapt and modify the content accordingly. Here are a few helpful suggestions to get you started.

If you have a wealth of expertise and you're applying for jobs in the same industry, list your experience first. For example, if you're a personal assistant applying for the same type of role, give a quick outline of your experience in a career profile at the beginning of the resume, followed by your IT skills, a detailed version of your work experience and educational qualifications.

A good way to conceal limited experience is to mesmerise the recruiter with your skills, abilities and achievements in a career summary at the beginning, followed by professional qualifications and academic accomplishments. Try to pull together any experience you've had and briefly mention the jobs; however, focus more on the transferable skills acquired.

Try to update your resume a few times a year. You never know when a great job will pop up, so take the pressure off and have your resume ready to go. You will still need to tailor your resume to each job role but by updating it a few times during the year, the task will take far less time and energy. You may like to keep a work diary throughout the year to record what you do on a regular basis. Make a note of any commendations or complimentary emails you receive as well as the details of your workplace successes. Also, when jotting down specific achievements, note the impact your good deeds had on the company. That way, when it comes to reviewing your resume you won't have to wrack your brains trying to recall your resume-worthy activities.

Part IV includes examples of resumes that bring to life everything we mention in this chapter: The essential ingredients and the optional extras.

Resume headings

Here are common section headings used in resumes. Consider using some of these when designing your own resume:

- Contact details
- Career objective
- Career goal
- Career summary
- Summary
- Profile
- Professional profile
- Career statement
- Capability statement
- Career highlights
- Achievements
- Education
- Courses
- Education and training
- Professional qualifications
- Qualifications
- Certifications
- Accomplishments

- Awards and honours
- Work experience
- Experience
- Employment
- Employment history
- Work history
- Part-time work
- Professional experience
- Projects
- Other experience
- Skills
- Key skills
- Skills summary
- Skills and expertise
- Professional skills
- Voluntary experience
- Community involvement
- University/community involvement
- Holiday work/internship

- Additional skills
- Technical skills
- Computer skills
- Software
- IT skills
- Extracurricular activities
- Languages
- Licences/registrations
- Training courses
- Professional development
- Professional memberships
- Memberships
- Memberships and associations
- Interests
- Interests and activities
- Activities
- Referees

Chapter 4

Winning Words for Resumes

. . . .

In This Chapter

▶ Using action verbs that stand out

▶ Showing your worth

▶ Filling your resume with the right keywords

. . . .

*W*ords are powerful. They can inspire, motivate and destroy. Words can communicate messages and convey emotions, feelings and ideas. They have the power to change your life and shape your experiences. Words sell your skills, abilities and achievements to a potential employer. Fill your resume with strong, powerful words that captivate interest and bring your resume to life.

In this chapter, we speak few words but provide you with an assortment of action verbs and templates, so you can master the skill of writing responsibilities and achievements. (Refer to Chapter 3 for specific details on how to incorporate these words in your resume.) We also talk about filling your e-resume with industry-specific keywords. This ensures your resume is easily discoverable when employers and recruiters are searching online databases for new recruits.

Actions Speak Louder than Words

When you're writing your resume, begin the sentences about your work experience and achievements with action verbs (refer to Chapter 3) that show the recruiter you can get results! Action verbs usually end in 'ed' and describe a particular task or action being performed. They make an impact and can add strength to your writing by promoting your work experience, skills and achievements in a positive and energetic manner. The following tables of action verbs help you create a powerful resume that grabs the attention of recruiters. Read through the lists of verbs and select those that add value and highlight your individual strengths. Try to avoid using the same word twice.

File away verbs for administration and office support

amended	drafted	prepared
answered	entered	processed
archived	established	produced
arranged	filed	purchased
assisted	followed up	reported
budgeted	generated	responded
checked	implemented	reviewed
collated	improved	scheduled
collected	liaised	screened
compiled	maintained	sorted
coordinated	monitored	supported
developed	ordered	typed
distributed	organised	updated
documented	planned	

Bargain verbs for customer service and retail

advertised	launched	publicised
balanced	maintained	purchased
budgeted	marked down	resolved
cashiered	maximised	rostered
closed	merchandised	served
communicated	motivated	sold
controlled	opened	stocked
counted	operated	stored
cross-sold	ordered	supervised
demonstrated	organised	trained
discounted	presented	transferred
displayed	priced	unpacked
exceeded	processed	up-sold
handled	promoted	welcomed

High-flying verbs for executives

achieved	developed	led
advised	directed	managed
analysed	disseminated	motivated
appointed	drafted	negotiated
approved	drove	oversaw
arbitrated	empowered	planned
assigned	engaged	produced
attained	executed	recommended
chaired	guided	reported
coached	headed	represented
collaborated	implemented	restructured
conceptualised	improved	reviewed
conducted	influenced	secured
consulted	initiated	supported
created	investigated	
delivered	launched	

On-the-money verbs for finance and accounting

adjusted	compiled	maintained
administrated	computed	prepared
allocated	decreased	processed
analysed	estimated	projected
assessed	financed	purchased
audited	finetuned	rationalised
banked	followed up	reconciled
budgeted	forecasted	recorded
bundled	funded	reduced
calculated	generated	reported
checked	invested	reviewed
collected	invoiced	

People-friendly verbs for human resources (HR)

advised	implemented	monitored
appraised	improved	negotiated
coached	inducted	organised
complied	initiated	recruited
conducted	instructed	reported
consulted	interpreted	resolved
counselled	interviewed	reviewed
created	investigated	screened
designed	launched	shortlisted
encouraged	liaised	supervised
evaluated	matched	supported
facilitated	mediated	transferred
hired	mentored	trained

Innovative verbs for information technology (IT)

analysed	integrated	programmed
assisted	interfaced	rebooted
computed	investigated	rebuilt
configured	launched	recovered
connected	logged	repaired
constructed	maintained	researched
consulted	modified	resolved
designed	monitored	restored
developed	operated	retrieved
diagnosed	organised	set up
implemented	performed	supported
initiated	printed	tested
installed	processed	upgraded

Helpful verbs for medical/healthcare

administered	diagnosed	nursed
attended	dispensed	performed
cared	educated	prescribed
comforted	examined	recorded
conducted	guided	referred
conferred	helped	rehabilitated
consoled	identified	reported
consulted	investigated	researched
counselled	measured	supplied
cured	monitored	x-rayed

Dynamite verbs for mining and construction

assessed	estimated	project-managed
built	excavated	repaired
calculated	extracted	reported
checked	identified	reviewed
constructed	implemented	scheduled
controlled	inspected	specified
coordinated	investigated	structured
delivered	maintained	supported
designed	measured	surveyed
drafted	monitored	tested
drilled	operated	undertook

Standout verbs for sales and marketing

achieved	generated	participated
advertised	identified	planned
communicated	influenced	presented
created	initiated	produced
cultivated	launched	promoted
delivered	liaised	proposed
demonstrated	maintained	represented
designed	marketed	researched
developed	motivated	reviewed
established	negotiated	secured
followed up	organised	

Educational verbs for teaching and training

adapted	developed	initiated
advised	directed	innovated
applied	displayed	instructed
assessed	distributed	lectured
clarified	educated	listened
coached	evaluated	maintained
communicated	facilitated	mentored
conducted	grouped	presented
coordinated	guided	summarised
delivered	identified	trained
demonstrated	implemented	tutored
designed	informed	

Handy verbs for technical and trades

assembled	maintained	picked
constructed	manufactured	processed
cut	mended	produced
examined	modified	rebuilt
fitted	moulded	scheduled
fixed	operated	serviced
inspected	ordered	solved
installed	packed	used
issued	painted	welded

Verbs for just about any job

accomplished	designed	invited
accumulated	detailed	issued
acted	devised	judged
addressed	disciplined	landscaped
adopted	downsized	logged
advanced	drafted	lowered
allocated	edited	mastered
amended	eliminated	matched
approved	encouraged	orchestrated
arbitrated	endorsed	oriented
arranged	enforced	outlined
assigned	enhanced	overcame
assured	ensured	oversaw
authored	entered	piloted
authorised	equipped	planned
booked	escalated	prioritised
catalogued	established	proofed
centralised	executed	proposed
checked	exhibited	publicised
circulated	facilitated	published
cleaned	financed	raised
collaborated	fitted	recommended
conformed	fixed	recorded
compared	formulated	rectified
completed	founded	reduced
composed	funded	registered
conceptualised	furnished	reserved
conducted	governed	rostered
cooked	guided	serviced
critiqued	headed	supplied
cultivated	hosted	surveyed
delegated	illustrated	welcomed
delivered	improved	wrote
designated	innovated	

Proving Your Achievements Made a Difference

When you write your achievements, impress the recruiter by highlighting not just what you've achieved but how you made a difference to your past employers' businesses. Here are a few time-saving templates that can take the pain out of constructing achievements from scratch. Fill in the blanks to showcase your top achievements.

Stating the facts

Improvements

Significantly reduced _____ by _____.

Launched a _____, which _____.

Reduced _____ by _____.

Streamlined processes and procedures, which _____.

Implemented a _____, which _____.

Creating/designing/developing something new

Designed a _____, which _____.

Created a _____.

Initiated and developed _____, which _____.

Redesigned _____, which _____.

Introduced a _____ that _____.

Developed a _____, which _____.

Productivity

Implemented a new _____ that increased workplace efficiency and productivity.

Increased productivity through _____.

Customer service

Increased customer satisfaction by _____.

Reduced customer complaints by _____.

Revenue

Increased revenue by _____.

Achievements/awards

Received numerous awards for outstanding customer service.

'Employee of the Month' for _____.

Awarded _____ for _____.

Received a _____ for _____.

Commended by management for _____.

Won _____ award for _____.

Earned _____.

Nominated by peers for _____.

Invited to attend _____.

Selected to _____.

Recognised for _____.

Stating the facts with numbers

Prove to recruiters how good you are by quantifying your achievements with numbers, percentages and dollar figures. Recruiters love high achievers, so why not broadcast the fact that you saved the company bucket-loads of money, increased sales by 50 per cent, doubled the customer base or boosted profits? Remember that using numbers is a great way for you to gain credibility in a recruiter's eyes. Here are some templates you can use to get started.

Customer service

Increased the customer base from _____ [#] to _____ [#] by _____.

Doubled the customer base in _____ [# years], as a result of _____.

Opened _____ [#] new accounts within a _____ [# month] period.

Achievements/awards

Won _____ award for _____ [#] consecutive years.

Selected from _____ [#] senior executives to represent the firm at a conference in Fiji.

Outstanding academic achievement with a Grade Point Average (GPA) of _____ [#].

Productivity

Increased _____ productivity by_____ % by _____.

Boosted _____ productivity from_____ % to _____ % by _____.

Streamlined _____ [system, process], increasing _____ productivity by _____ %.

Profits

Increased profits by _____ % through_____.

Developed and implemented a _____, increasing profits by _____ %.

Sales

Increased sales from $_____ to $_____ by _____.

Generated sales in excess of $_____ annually through _____.

Initiated a _____ [name of campaign, program], which increased sales by $_____.

Costs/expenses

Streamlined production processes saving $_____ in costs annually.

Renegotiated supplier contracts saving the company $_____ each year.

Reduced operating expenses from $_____ to $_____ as a result of _____.

Restructured _____ resulting in a cost saving for the department of $_____.

Saved the company $_____ by _____.

Revenue

Launched a _____ campaign, increasing revenue from $_____ to over $_____ a year.

Developed _____ [program], which generated $_____ in annual revenue.

Using Industry-Specific Keywords

When large companies and recruitment agencies have openings to fill, they often search their own databases first to retrieve resumes by performing a keyword search. Keywords are nouns, short phrases, buzzwords, industry jargon or occupational terminology that the recruiter uses to narrow their search for people with the skills and qualifications they're after. For example, if the recruiter is looking for a customer service representative, they might type **customer service representative** or **call centre** into the search box for the database. The trick is to fill your resume with the right keywords so that it automatically gets picked up when the employer searches the database. We also talk about choosing keywords in Chapter 3.

Unfortunately, you won't find a universal list that outlines every single keyword for your industry. Each recruiter types in their own keywords depending upon the job and skills required. However, job ads provide lots of keywords and professional social media platform LinkedIn also has a feature that allows you to find the most commonly used terms for a particular job role and industry. We talk more about using social media platforms in Chapter 8.

The following lists provide you with examples of keywords for different industries.

Keywords for accounting

accounts payable	financial controller
accounts receivable	invoicing
assistant accountant	management accountant
bookkeeping	payroll
CA, CPA	taxation
financial accountant	

Keywords for administration/ office support

admin assistant

advanced Microsoft Office

attention to detail

data entry

deadline driven

diary/email management

executive assistant

HR administrator

initiative

organisational skills

personal assistant

receptionist

records management

secretary

strong communication skills

team administrator

travel coordinator

Keywords for customer service

call centre

cash handling

cashier

collections

cross-sell

customer assistant

customer loyalty

customer relationship management

customer retention

customer service

customer service representative

customer service team leader

face-to-face retail

inbound

outbound

sales

sales assistant

sales targets

service quality

telemarketing

teller

Keywords for human resources (HR)

change management

employee relations

generalist

HR adviser

HR manager/HR officer/HR business partner

HRIS

industrial relations

knowledge management

organisational development

payroll

performance management

recruitment/onboarding/induction

remuneration and benefits

retention

staffing

strategic planning

succession planning

talent management

training

workplace health and safety/OHS

Keywords for industrial/trades

apprenticeship

arc welding

boilermaker

CNC machining

CNC programming

dockhand

forklift drivers

general machining

heavy diesel

maintenance work

MIG welding

mine operator

plastics tooling work

press tool work

process worker

shutdown work

TIG welding

tool making

truck driver

Keywords for information technology (IT)

application development/support

business development

CCNA/CCNP/CCIE/CCDP/CCDA

database

engineer

helpdesk

J2EE

MCSE

MCP

VB

network

Oracle/SQL

project management

system administration

system analysis

system implementation

testing

Unix

Windows

Keywords for sales/marketing

above the line

advertising

B2B (business to business)

B2C (business to consumer)

below the line

brand management

campaign

category management (or manager)

direct marketing/direct response

investor relations

loyalty marketing/programs

market research

marketing sales analyst

marketing manager

product manager

promotions/events

retail marketing

social media marketing

social networking

sponsorship

Chapter 5

Overcoming Resume Dilemmas

• •

In This Chapter

▶ Repairing resume problems

▶ Dealing with a change in direction

▶ Re-entering the workforce

▶ Dealing with employment barriers

• •

*T*his chapter is the DIY guide to painting, patching and covering over common resume problems. We show you how to deal with career cracks and blemishes due to unemployment, retrenchment and mergers; how to make your recent sea change look good on paper; how to protect yourself against discrimination due to age or disability; and how to represent time out through parenting, study or illness.

Career gaps are fairly common these days. Most people take breaks from work to travel, raise a family, study, try to find work, change careers, care for a sick relative or recover from an illness. The good thing about career gaps is that they're easy to fix with a little bit of handiwork and know-how. In this chapter, we present you with hints, tools, techniques and tips to overcome resume dilemmas and help you create a polished, seamless masterpiece.

Pasting Over the Cracks

Are you struggling to make your resume look good because of employment holes? Perhaps you've been travelling, chopped and changed jobs a lot or been retrenched an unfortunate amount of times. Don't panic — chances are you're only in need of a minor resume repair.

Dealing with career gaps

The good news for you is that most recruiters acknowledge that holes in a work history are a reality in today's world. Here are ways you can deal with gaps.

Sealing up the holes by using years only

If you have a gap of one year or less, caulk up the crack by detailing only the years of employment in your work history. We give an example in Figure 5-1. Notice how the career gap mysteriously disappears like magic.

This technique is a temporary quick fix. You may be required to verify the months and years of employment during the job interview, so be prepared to volunteer this information and discuss the gap then.

Original resume

Administration Officer   **January 2012–Present**
Department of Employment & Job Prospects

Executive Assistant   **August 2009–June 2011**
Department of Go-Getters

Note the gap from July 2011–December 2011

Revised resume

Administration Officer   **2012–Present**
Department of Employment & Job Prospects

Executive Assistant   **2009–2011**
Department of Go-Getters

Ta da! The gap is no longer visible

Figure 5-1: Disguising a career gap by using years only.

Never lie about employment gaps or fudge employment dates. Recruiters often have ways of discovering this information by looking at your social media profiles and through referee checking. The last thing you need is a black cross against your name and a question mark on your integrity. Honesty is the best policy.

Saying nothing

Some HR professionals and career development practitioners recommend leaving career gaps — particularly ones that may be perceived negatively. Figure 5-2 shows you an example of how to omit information from your resume work history. The downside to this is that it raises speculation and may cause the recruiter to wonder what's been happening to you during this period.

Being honest

The third approach requires you to be honest, stating the reasons for the gaps in your career history. This alleviates suspicion and shows the recruiter or employer you've got nothing to hide. See Figure 5-3 for an example of how you can account for a travel gap, for example, in your work history. You can take the same approach to explain taking a career break to raise children.

Legal Secretary   **September 2013–Present**
Rich, Richer & Richest Partners in Law

Legal Secretary   **March 2009–September 2011**
Jackson & Jackson Solicitors

Figure 5-2: Leaving a career gap in your resume.

Pharmacist   **May 2010–Present**
Jill Pill's Pharmacy

Overseas travel   **October 2008–April 2010**

Pharmacist   **March 2004–September 2008**
Tom White Chemists

Figure 5-3: Accounting for overseas travel in your resume.

Using the word 'present' to hide the gap

If you've been unemployed for less than a month, some people recommend plugging up the gap by putting the date you started your most recent role and then '– Present'. This gives the recruiter the impression that you're currently employed. In Figure 5-4, even though the job applicant quit in November 2014 and it's now December 2014, it looks as if they've still been working (and not sitting poolside in the Whitsundays).

Interior Designer *Designs R Us*	**October 2013–Present**
Interior Designer *Classic Designs*	**March 2007–September 2013**

Figure 5-4: Masking a gap using the word 'Present'.

Be warned. Employers don't look favourably upon deception. Be prepared to justify your actions in an interview or after the interview when the recruiter validates your employment details in a referee check. Remember, first impressions do count.

An alternative is to write in the finishing date of your most recent job and cover over the gap using an employment filler such as temporary work. Again, never lie and pretend you have worked when you haven't.

Managing repeated retrenchments

The average person will be retrenched up to three times in their career; however, with fast-changing global economic conditions, that number could increase. If you've been retrenched multiple times, perhaps you've been walking under too many ladders or have the uncanny knack of being in the wrong place at the wrong time.

In most instances, the circumstances leading to redundancy are beyond your control. For example, the company you were working for went belly up or merged with another organisation — the best course of action is to outline the reasons for leaving in your resume. Explain why your role was made redundant — and if your role was one of a number to go, mention this too. This takes the onus off you and allays any fears a potential employer may have about your work performance. Figure 5-5 shows you how these circumstances can be outlined in your resume.

Human Resource Manager   **March 2009–February 2013**
SmartChoice Health Funds

Responsibilities

Achievements

Reasons for leaving: Company closed down, and the roles of all 110 staff were made redundant.

Human Resource officer   **October 2005–December 2008**
Medico Insurance

Responsibilities

Achievements

Reasons for leaving: Company relocated its HR operations to Sydney. My role was made redundant along with the roles of six other Melbourne-based HR team members.

Human Resource Coordinator   **January 2005–September 2005**
Insurance Plus

Responsibilities

Achievements

Reasons for leaving: Company downsized its operations after a challenging financial year, resulting in the loss of five job roles, including mine.

Figure 5-5: Dealing with multiple retrenchments.

Manipulating mergers and acquisitions

A merger or acquisition occurs when a parent company takes over or acquires another company to form a new firm with the intention of gaining a strategic edge in the market. If you've been working in one organisation for a long period of time, you may have witnessed a number of corporate mergers or acquisitions. The challenge for you is how to list these changes of ownership in your resume so that a recruiter gains a good understanding of what's been going on in your work history.

'Fessing up to being fired

If only life were as simple as being able to say, 'I told my boss to go jump in the lake and he fired me.' If you've been sacked fairly or unfairly, don't hide the fact behind a smoke screen. (Never get into the habit of making derogatory remarks about past employers either. This reflects badly on you and creates a poor impression in the interview.)

If you have been fired, save all explanations for the interview. Keep your resume brief and controversy-free and avoid including details on why you left previous jobs. Don't get defensive when the issue is raised during the interview; calmly justify what happened. More often than not, if you have been given the boot it's generally due to a personal conflict rather than a performance issue. Most recruiters acknowledge the fact that personality clashes happen and with a bit of luck won't automatically wipe your job prospects as a result. On the other hand, if your performance was the problem, you may need to say a few prayers, and ensure your past referees will sing your praises.

Same company, different jobs, two mergers

The most practical way to deal with multiple mergers and acquisitions if you've been with the same firm and had different jobs is to list each change separately, outlining your job titles, responsibilities and achievements. Don't forget to substantiate any changes of ownership in brackets. This makes it clear and easy for an employer to track the changes. We show an example in Figure 5-6.

Senior Accountant   **January 2011–Present**
HDS International (formerly Hamilton & Douglas Worldwide)

Accountant   **May 2004–December 2010**
Hamilton & Douglas Worldwide (formerly Hamilton & Associates)

Assistant Accountant   **June 2001–April 2004**
Hamilton & Associates

Figure 5-6: Dealing with multiple mergers and acquisitions when you have different jobs.

Same company, same job, two mergers

When it comes to multiple mergers and acquisitions where you have held the one position, list your job title, current company name, responsibilities and achievements once, then provide the recruiter with a short explanation of the merger and acquisition changes as demonstrated in Figure 5-7.

Payroll Officer   July 2010–Present
HDS International

(Hamilton & Associates, the original parent company I worked for, undertook a series of mergers and acquisitions to become Hamilton Douglas Worldwide and the current entity HDS International.)

Figure 5-7: Dealing with multiple mergers and acquisitions when you've kept the same job.

Add the details of the history behind any mergers and acquisitions in your resume. Don't take the easy option of leaving it up to recruiters to discover the fact themselves.

Covering up your job-hopping

If you have a history of moving from one job to another within a relatively short period of time, recruiters may stereotype you as a *job-hopper*. Some of the most common reasons for job-hopping are

- The organisation closes down

- The firm acquires or merges with another company

- The company moves its operations to a new location

- The position or function within a department dissolves and is absorbed in the business elsewhere

- The owner of the business retires

- Temporary employment, contract or short-term project work

- A job incumbent returns to their permanent public sector role after a leave of absence, travel, maternity leave or secondment to another department

- Relocation (interstate or overseas)

- Poor performance

- Limited career progression and development opportunities

- Personality conflicts with managers or staff

- Misconduct or dishonesty

- Health reasons

Job-hopping is considered the norm in some industries. If you're a tradesperson, for example, or a contract engineer, changing jobs and having short bursts of employment is common. For example, when times are good in the IT sector, employers often use a great number of contractors and even pay them at a higher rate. However, moods can change, and when a business goes through challenging times, employers often avoid those with a long history of contracting and favour those who have been in permanent jobs.

Some recruiters will look negatively on your mish-mash of short-term jobs and you may be disadvantaged when compared to other candidates with equal qualifications but stable work histories. Unfortunately, job-hopping can conjure up images that you may be unstable, disloyal, unreliable, incompetent or a potential troublemaker.

Whether this is true or not you need to create the best impression and win over the recruiter right from the word go.

Here are a few tips and tricks to help you overcome a job-hopping image.

- ✓ **Demonstrate to the employer that you're an excellent worker.** Reduce recruiter anxiety and dispel any myths by advertising the fact you're an achiever and a top performer. Display awards, highlight your promotions and litter your resume with achievements — written or verbal commendations from managers or clients always look good. Market the fact you're flexible, you thrive on change, you're adaptable to new working environments and have amassed a repertoire of skills they need. Show the recruiter you can make a difference.

- ✓ **Display reasons for leaving jobs in your work history.** This is helpful particularly in cases where you were the unfortunate victim of circumstance such as a company closure. This clarifies the job gap and shows the employer you didn't leave on bad terms. See Figure 5-8 for an example of how to present this on your resume.

Whatever you do, don't bombard a recruiter or employer with negative reasons for leaving a job. Announcing you left an organisation due to poor performance, were sacked, or quit because of a personal conflict does little to inspire faith in your abilities and may brand you as a dud. As a general rule, if the reason is negative don't mention it at all in your resume.

Process Worker *ABC Foods*	**March 2012–October 2013**

Responsibilities
- Operated and maintained a packing machine
- Loaded and refilled packaging
- Tested and inspected machinery, recording faults and equipment malfunctions in a log book
- Stamped and dated biscuit packaging
- Checked biscuits were within tolerance for defects
- Maintained the factory's cleanliness and hygiene standards

Achievements
- Trained staff in operational procedures that increased production output from 1000 packaged biscuits per minute to 1200 per minute.

Reason for leaving: Company closure

Figure 5-8: Demonstrating a reason for leaving a job.

Putting together a patchwork career

Is your career like a patchwork quilt, comprising bits and pieces of work experience stitched together in a haphazard manner? If you've had a pattern of changing careers regularly, threading together the relevant work experience from each of your roles and tailoring the resume to the job you're applying for is important. If you've had a patchy career, the trick to sewing up a winning resume is to emphasise and de-emphasise jobs.

Know that you're not alone. The average person leaving school this year has three or more careers to look forward to over their working life. Other trends occurring nowadays include the 'slashie' career, also known as the 'and' career or 'portfolio' career. This is where a person has more than one type of job role simultaneously: For example, corporate trainer/dog groomer/bookkeeper. People are juggling more than one career at a time for many reasons, including a lack of job security and a greater focus on lifelong learning.

It pays to be multi-skilled and even multi-qualified. While this trend is growing in popularity among Australians and New Zealanders, employers will always be looking for people with experience and a proven track record in a particular skill area, so be prepared to tailor your resume to every job you apply for.

Sounding too good to be true

Sometimes you have bucket-loads of qualifications and experience, but still struggle to find work. Even if you are well educated with a PhD and an MBA, you run the risk of being labelled as overqualified if you're applying for lower-paid positions. Sounds crazy, but some recruiters or employers fear if you have too many qualifications you may get bored in the job and be inclined to take something else bigger and better and move on within a short period of time. You need to convince a potential employer that this is not the case and you genuinely want the job. Here are some simple strategies:

- Check what qualifications are required. Don't paint yourself into a corner by listing your PhD and masters qualifications for every job you're applying for. Only include the qualifications that are required for the job. A PhD or a masters degree may be brushed aside as intimidating and too costly.

- Communicate your qualifications within the same industry. If you've updated your qualifications in the same field or industry, plaster your resume with your newly acquired doctorate or masters degree. This demonstrates your academic prowess and shows your commitment to climbing the ladder of learning. For senior and line management roles, postgraduate qualifications are often viewed favourably, so if you've got it, why not flaunt it?

- Don't list all the work experience you've acquired in your resume. Focus on your most recent jobs and try to go back no further than ten years. This can be tricky if you've only had one job in ten years. In such cases, go back a bit further or set out the separate roles you held at the one organisation during the past ten years to show your career progression. Remember, broadcasting all your experience is like advertising your age on a billboard. That said, with many employers now searching to see if you have a social media profile on platforms such as LinkedIn or Facebook, employers can view a photo of you fairly easily. However, resumes should only list the information that is relevant to the role, so chances are that the job you had 20 years ago has no bearing on the one you're applying for today.

- If you've been with just one company in one role, alleviate any fears or perceptions a recruiter may have of you in terms of lacking drive and energy. Show the potential employer that while you may have been in the same role for eons, you're really self-motivated, love learning and are highly skilled. Highlight in your resume any professional associations you're a member of, list professional development courses you've attended and document evidence of taking on additional responsibility in the company.

- Dispel any myths of being rigid by outlining any improvements or changes you've made to existing procedures, processes or systems.

Consider this scenario: You've had five years' experience as a nurse, three years' work in retail sales as an assistant manager and two years' experience selling property. You want to apply for a position as a real estate sales consultant — what do you do?

Don't go into unnecessary detail, listing achievements and responsibilities for past roles that have no relevance to the job you're applying for.

You need to highlight the relevant experience and downplay the rest. For example, in the scenario outlined in this section, going into too much detail about your nursing experience would be foolish, because it doesn't relate to real estate. With regards to your assistant manager role, you could tie in the fact that you cross-sold and up-sold products to customers and exceeded sales targets. Because you've had two years of relevant work experience in real estate, which is particularly important to this role, it makes sense to list your responsibilities and achievements for this job in your resume.

Having previous experience as a nurse and in retail is a huge plus for a real estate sales consultant role: You'd have dealt with people from all walks of life and had to gain their trust, so look out for the transferable skills provided by previous careers. See the next section for more on transferable skills.

Making Your Change of Career Look Good

Every time you switch careers and take onboard a new change, you face the inevitable prospect of having no experience under your belt. Employers generally like work experience, so the biggest challenge entering a new field is how to promote yourself in your resume while disguising the fact you have no experience.

If you've had a dramatic career change, consider using a career profile and/or a list of key skills at the top of your resume to highlight any additional relevant skills gained over your career. You may also wish to include a career objective in your resume to advise the recruiter of your career intentions and clarify your future career goals. We talk more about career profiles, career objectives and key skills lists in Chapter 3.

Here are some useful tips to help you survive the changing of lanes:

- ✓ **Participate in networking activities.** Join associations and industry groups to network with professionals and key contacts in the industry. They've travelled down the same path in the past and may offer you a few pointers on how to make roads into the industry. Make sure you're enthusiastic, friendly and give off positive signals; you may even score a job in the process. Don't forget to list the association or industry group in your resume. Networking can also be a great way to discover new job opportunities, where the person offering the job is sold on you first and your job history later — the opposite of applying for advertised jobs.

- ✓ **Find a mentor.** Look for someone with knowledge and experience in the industry. Mentors are like road maps; they guide you to where you want to go and highlight the best route to travel. They also know people!

- ✓ **Highlight your transferable skills.** Skills can be grouped into three main categories: Technical, people-related and transferable. Technical skills are job-related skills that are specific to a particular occupation or profession. For example, to be an auditor you need audit skills, an architectural technician requires drafting skills and so on. People-related skills refers to your personal attributes, qualities or character traits, such as being honest, loyal, reliable, enthusiastic and self-motivated. Transferable skills are generic skills you've acquired in the past that can be applied to any job. Communication, problem-solving and interpersonal skills are all examples of transferable skills that are used in lots of different industries — journalism, sales, administration, HR, retail, public relations . . . the list goes on and on.

Stop and think about any transferable skills you've acquired through volunteer work, paid employment, parenting, study, hobbies and sports that could be applied to your new career. For example, if you're transitioning from a teaching job into the human resources profession (training), you may draw attention to the fact you were teaching students, planning lessons and developing resources. Training, planning and communication skills are all important in a HR role. Similarly, if you're wishing to enter the events management field and have been working in administration, highlight your experience coordinating the staff Christmas party for 100 staff and arranging business forums and conferences. Again, you're matching the skills you have to the new career field.

So how do you go about recognising and developing a list of your transferable skills? Here's how:

1. **Make a list of all transferable skills you've acquired through study, hobbies, sports and paid and unpaid employment.**

   You can see examples of transferable skills in Table 5-1.

2. **Find out what skills are required for the job you're applying for. You can do this by scanning the advertisement or skimming the job description for clues.**

3. **Tick off any transferable skills that match to the job.**

4. **Use your list to play up your transferable skills in your resume in your career profile, list of key skills and/or in the responsibilities and achievements sections for relevant jobs in your resume.**

   See Figure 5-9 for an example.

Table 5-1   Examples of Transferable Skills

Skill Set	Job Skills
Communication	Listening, writing, negotiating, facilitating, teaching, interviewing, influencing, persuading, reporting, selling, expressing ideas, networking, editing, public speaking, telephone techniques
Computer/ technology	Keyboarding, spreadsheeting, data entry, word processing, emailing, searching, using the Internet
Interpersonal	Building rapport, empathising, teamwork counselling
Management/ leadership	Mentoring, coaching, delegating, motivating staff, instructing, supervising, inspiring, leading, accepting responsibility, directing, managing conflict, decision-making
Organisation/ planning	Coordinating, arranging, planning, prioritising, meeting deadlines, setting goals, following up, handling multiple tasks, managing time, attention to detail, scheduling
Problem solving	Analysing, evaluating alternatives, lateral thinking, proposing a solution, reviewing
Research/ investigation	Gathering facts, examining data, extracting and summarising information, identifying, interpreting, synthesising
Teamwork	Sharing, helping, collaborating, supporting, cooperating, compromising, respecting others, contributing ideas

Step 1: Make a list of the skills you've acquired in your past job/s
Executive Assistant
- Screened telephone calls
- Diary management/scheduled appointments
- Drafted correspondence on behalf of the general manager
- Organised meetings, conferences and events — senior executive forum, executive team meetings, staff Christmas party
- Coordinated travel and accommodation bookings
- Prepared routine correspondence — letters, memos, minutes, agendas
- Maintained office equipment
- Ordered office supplies
- Created invitations, PowerPoint presentations and flyers

Step 2: Make a list of the skills required for the job you're applying for
Events Coordinator at Company B
- Organisational skills — multi-tasking capabilities, time management, planning, coordination, attention to detail
- Communication skills (written and oral)
- Interpersonal skills
- Administration skills
- Computing skills (Word, Excel, Access, PowerPoint)
- Customer service skills
- Ability to work independently
- Creative

Step 3: Tick off any skills that relate to the new role
- Screened telephone calls
- Diary management/scheduled appointments
- Drafted correspondence on behalf on the General Manager
- Organised meetings, conferences and events — senior executive forum, executive team meetings, staff Christmas party ✓
- Coordinated travel and accommodation bookings ✓
- Prepared routine correspondence — letters, memos, minutes, agendas
- Maintained office equipment
- Ordered office supplies ✓
- Created invitations, PowerPoint presentations, handouts and flyers ✓

Step 4: Use these transferable skills in your resume
Career Profile
Highly organised with well-developed time management skills. Experienced in coordinating quarterly forums for up to 150 senior executives. Executed every aspect of the event from planning through to troubleshooting at the event itself.

Key Skills
- Negotiating supplier agreements
- Choosing and booking venues
- Sourcing and securing guest speakers
- Creating invitations for the event

And so on.

Figure 5-9: Focusing on transferable skills.

Here are a couple of additional things you can do to impress a recruiter:

- ✔ **Undertake some voluntary work.** If the market you're entering is low demand but saturated with a high number of qualified candidates with direct experience in the field, you may need to do some work experience in the area for a temporary period of time. Unpaid work will give you some basic skills and knowledge to put in your resume.

- ✔ **Compose a cover letter outlining the reasons for your move.** Design a well-constructed cover letter that delves into your motives for changing careers. Employers then have an idea of your background and motivations. Keep this succinct and straight to the point and try not to waffle. We talk more about cover letters in Chapter 7.

Gearing Up for Re-Entry

If you've been absent from the workforce for a long period of time due to raising a family, a period of illness, caring for a sick relative or study, you need to spice up your resume to successfully re-enter the workforce. With carefully worded phrases you can turn your career lowlights into highlights.

Raising a family

If you've taken time out from your career to raise kids, you know it's a full-time job. You oughta be congratulated! In this section, we show you how making the transition back into the workforce need not be daunting.

Highlight what you have to offer by creating a career profile and/ or list of key skills and placing this near the top of your resume to attract attention right off the bat.

Recruiters and employers want to run their eye down the work history section of your resume and see an uninterrupted timeline. Rather than leave a gap in your resume, create a job-style entry to cover the time you spent raising a family. Use a professional heading instead of 'housewife' or 'househusband' and include the relevant dates like we have in the following examples:

Family Commitments, April 2008 – February 2013

Full-time parent, December 2009 – January 2012

Under the heading place information about the relevant skills you developed during this period. See Figure 5-10 for an example layout.

Secretary of the Parents & Citizens Association (P&C).

Responsibilities: Driving fundraising events, preparing agendas, distributing minutes, scheduling meetings, updating and maintaining records, typing correspondence.

Skills acquired: People management, time management, organisational skills, administration.

Achievements:
- Raised $12,000 for the P&C by organising a school talent competition night including securing a well-known MC.
- Increased canteen sales by 20% through initiating and developing a healthy foods campaign for primary school children.

Figure 5-10: An example resume entry to demonstrate skills acquired while raising a family.

Here are some suggestions for ways to describe what you've been doing during your tenure as full-time mum, cook and bottlewasher, to include in your resume:

✔ **Listing volunteer or community work.** Demonstrate to a recruiter that while you haven't held a paid job, you've still acquired a suite of valuable skills.

✔ **Assisting in the running of a business owned by your spouse.** You may have performed the bookkeeping, provided admin support, dealt with customers or liaised with suppliers. Don't be shy. Include this detail.

✔ **Quantifying achievements.** Don't just highlight what volunteer or unpaid work you performed but show the recruiter how you made a difference to the community, school or organisation you worked for.

✔ **Pulling together your home-based skills.** If you have not held roles outside the home, you could still provide a concise summary of some of the skills you acquired while raising your child or children. While some recruiters question the value of such skills, others view them as legitimate transferable skills that can be passed from one job to another. Some examples are:

- **Managed the family finances:** Budgeting.

- **Multi-tasking, time management, organisational skills:** Managing the cleaning and operation of the home while also running errands, taking children to activities and sports and liaising with a range of suppliers from retailers to tradespeople to school staff.

- **Resolved interpersonal conflicts within family:** Conflict resolution skills.

- **Fixed problems within the home:** Problem solving.

Covering up a criminal record

There are times for telling the truth, the whole truth and nothing but the truth; then there are times to be discreet. If you have a criminal record, writing your resume is a time to be discreet. Don't attract attention to past misdemeanours — your resume is meant to win over the recruiter by portraying you in the best possible light. Avoid becoming a career casualty and don't list negatives on your resume that do you no justice.

If you have committed a serious offence, avoid looking for work in industries where your previous conviction makes you seem a risk to hire. No recruiter wants to hire an accountant whose past includes embezzling money from corporate accounts. Your best option is to change careers and start afresh, using networking or agencies that help those who have been in prison find an employer who will give them a go.

Some government departments and private sector organisations require you to complete an application form, consenting to a criminal history check as a prerequisite to employment. Procedures will vary depending on where you are looking for work. In some cases you will be required to lodge an application form in person at your local police station with proof of ID. Alternatively, you may be asked to retrieve the form online or from a police station, complete the relevant sections, then lodge it online with supporting attachments or post it with supporting documents to a particular agency for processing. Be prepared to incur a small administration fee for the service. Once your record appears on the police certificate, the recruiter will need to make a full and informed assessment of your suitability for the role. Be prepared for oodles of questions and being hauled over the coals. One way around this is to apply for jobs where criminal history checks are not undertaken.

If you're returning to the same career you left, get up to speed with what's been going on in your industry; things will have changed in your absence. This means renewing professional memberships, doing refresher courses, attending networking events, reading industry magazines and journals, and touching base with old work contacts.

Recovering from an illness

Sickness can strike you down at any moment. Be warned, while laws exist preventing employers discriminating against candidates on the basis of a previous illness or ongoing disability, most employers will never tell you the reason they did not give you the job. If you spell out that you have been ill on your resume with limited explanation, red flags may go up for the HR manager or recruiter, fearing you could be a liability if hired. Employers tend to think the worst and may associate an illness with low productivity and extended absences. The best thing to do is to leave any evidence of sickness out of your resume.

If you've experienced an illness that caused a prolonged absence from the world of work, the best remedy is to be honest and tell the employer the truth in person at the interview. This way, you can explain how you've made a full recovery or how you manage your health and thus alleviate any fears the recruiter may have about your current health and future work capabilities.

Caring for a loved one

If you've been a noble soul caring for a terminally ill parent or relative, you will need to account for this gap in your resume. The best approach is to be honest, stating in a brief sentence what's been happening during your period of unemployment. Figure 5-11 shows you how to present this on your resume. You can even outline the skills you developed in this time.

Taking time off to study

When dealing with a study gap, account for the black hole by stating the qualifications you attained, the institution or college where you studied and the year the course was completed under a professional qualifications heading in your resume (refer to Chapter 3). If a gap exists in your work history, recruiters will examine the professional qualifications section and piece the jigsaw parts together. Otherwise, clarify the job gap with a simple explanation such as 'Full-time study'.

Home carer for mother   **July 2002–December 2002**

Responsibilities: Liaised with medical and healthcare practitioners, provided and arranged transport and managed all the financial affairs during this period.

Registered Nurse   **February 2000–June 2002**
Prince Arthur Hospital

Figure 5-11: Closing the gap — caring for an ill relative.

Avoiding Being Discriminated Against

Employers are acting illegally if they discriminate against someone on the basis of age, gender, race, pregnancy, colour, religion, disability, nationality, marital status and sexual preference. In Australia, separate acts comprising both state and federal legislation protect you from being disadvantaged when applying for jobs, as well as in the workplace.

To see a full list of these areas of discrimination, go to the Australian Human Rights Commission website: www.humanrights.gov.au/guide-australias-anti-discrimination-laws.

The website for the Human Rights Commission in New Zealand features an even longer list of areas of discrimination. These include age, colour, disability, race, marital status, employment status, sexual orientation, family status, ethnic belief and political opinion. You can learn more about these areas of discrimination by visiting: www.hrc.co.nz/enquiries-and-complaints-guide/areas-of-public-life/discriminatory-laws.

Table 5-2 gives you an indication of unacceptable and discriminatory behaviour in the workplace.

Table 5-2	Examples of Workplace Discrimination
Type of Discrimination	*Example*
Gender	A man is not considered for a part-time role even though he's the best person for the job because it's assumed he's really wanting a full-time position and will leave as soon as he finds one.
Race	A person of Asian descent is not considered for a position as marketing executive because the manager thinks the non-Asian customers will not be comfortable dealing with him.
Disability	A wheelchair user can't enter a building because the only means of entry is via stairs and no access to a lift/ ramp is available.
Age	An employee is made redundant because he or she is considered to be too old to understand new technology to be used in the area.
Physical appearance	An applicant is rejected because they're very short.
Marital status	A married woman is not interviewed for a position because her husband works for the same organisation in a similar role.
Breastfeeding	A woman's request to have a lock installed on a meeting-room door, blinds fixed on the windows to allow privacy and access to a fridge to store her expressed milk is refused without consideration.
Pregnancy	A woman who has applied for a promotion while pregnant is not considered for the position because it's assumed that she will not want to return to work full-time, and no consideration is given to how the position could be done on a job-share or part-time basis.
Parental or carer status	A parent takes carer's leave and is subject to snide comments about the leave because team members without children think the employee is getting a benefit that they don't get.
Sexual orientation	A gay man is overlooked for selection into a role when he's clearly the best person for the job because the supervisor is uncomfortable with homosexuality.
Political belief or activity	A person's progressive political beliefs aren't tolerated in a conservative office.

Industrial belief or activity	A union organiser is constantly overlooked for performance rewards despite being the highest achiever in the team.
Racial vilification	An ethnic employee is called 'wog' by a fellow employee.
Return from maternity leave	A woman returning to work from maternity leave has her salary and role title maintained but the value of the new client group she's responsible for is only a tenth of the value of her pre-maternity leave client group.
Sexual harassment	When showing his two young female staff members how to use the new computer program, the male supervisor stands very close to them and leans over their shoulders.

If you feel you have been discriminated against unlawfully during a recruitment process, you may wish to lodge a formal complaint. Discrimination complaints can be directed to the Australian Human Rights Commission on (02) 9284 9600. Alternatively each state has its own jurisdiction to deal with discrimination and harassment cases. In New Zealand, you can contact the Human Rights Commission on 0800 496 877 (toll free).

The following list provides website addresses that provide information and contact details:

- **ACT Human Rights Commission:** www.hrc.act.gov.au

- **Anti-Discrimination Board of New South Wales** www.antidiscrimination.lawlink.nsw.gov.au

- **Northern Territory Anti-Discrimination Commission:** www.adc.nt.gov.au/

- **Anti-Discrimination Commission Queensland:** www.adcq.qld.gov.au

- **Equal Opportunity Commission of South Australia:** www.eoc.sa.gov.au

- **Office of the Anti-Discrimination Commissioner (Tasmania):** www.antidiscrimination.tas.gov.au

- ✔ **Victorian Equal Opportunity and Human Rights Commission**: www.humanrightscommission.vic. gov.au

- ✔ **Equal Opportunity Commission Western Australia**: www.eoc.wa.gov.au

Ageing gracefully

We're going to be incredibly blunt now: Age can be an obstacle if you let it be. There's no denying the fact that some employers are ageist. While legislation makes it illegal to discriminate on the basis of age, some recruiters and hiring managers will find any excuse to eliminate older workers from their shortlist.

Even being 35 can be considered 'too old' in some sectors and job roles, and someone aged 45 or over is considered a 'mature age worker'. Here are a few tactics to help you disguise your age and show recruiters and employers that you're not too far over the hill:

- ✔ **Highlight the benefits of your knowledge and expertise in your resume.** Promote your maturity, loyalty and expertise to a potential employer and use this as a marketing ploy over younger job seekers to get jobs. Submit your resume to recruiters who may benefit from your skills and knowledge, such as a new or developing company venturing into unchartered waters. You may be a 'golden oldie' but you still have experience on your side! Milk it to your advantage.

- ✔ **Avoid detailing every position you have held.** If your work history dates back to the disco era, don't go overboard and list every job and every employer you've ever worked for. Concentrate on your recent experience and most relevant jobs and go back no more than ten years. Your resume should show a potential employer you're well qualified rather than well preserved.

- ✔ **Stay relevant.** Prove to the recruiter you're up-to-date by filling your resume with the latest industry buzzwords and terms.

- ✔ **Woo the recruiter with your technological proficiency.** Some recruiters have the perception that older workers are slower to learn new computer tricks and are all technophobes. Dispel this myth by sending your resume online and keeping up to date with the latest software packages and developments. Ensure your resume includes the technology you're proficient in, as well as your social media skills, any relevant blogs you contribute to and all your recent training and certifications. This shows off your skills and knowledge, plus your willingness to continually learn and develop.

✓ **Omit your age, date of birth and the year you graduated from your educational qualifications.** Eliminating any resume details that will give the recruiter a clue to your age is always wise. Keep yourself a mystery and leave no traceable evidence for the Sherlock Holmes recruiter. It's elementary, my dear Watson!

Here are a few websites well worth checking out if you are a mature-age job seeker:

✓ **Adage** (www.adage.com.au): The job board where experience matters. Australia's leading career centre and employment website for mature age professionals aged 45+. Free to job seekers.

✓ **Jobwise** (www.jobwise.gov.au): An Australian government site promoting mature-age employment. Great source of information for both employers and job seekers.

✓ **Older Workers** (www.olderworkers.com.au): An Australian job board for mature age workers listing jobs and providing job hunting resources.

✓ **Plus40** (www.plus40.com.au): This website offers services to both job hunters over 40 and employers looking for mature age workers.

For more mature New Zealanders, go to the government website www.careers.govt.nz and type 'mature age worker' into the search box to access all the pages for older job hunters.

Disclosing a disability

The Australian Commonwealth *Disabilities Discrimination Act 1992* and state government anti-discrimination and equal opportunity legislation protect disabled workers from being treated less favourably on the basis of a disability. While this is a safeguard for you, it never guarantees that unscrupulous employers won't weasel around the law to find an excuse to add you to the rejection pile.

Here are some tips to keep in mind if you do have a disability:

- ✔ **Avoid listing your disability on your resume.** Don't divert unnecessary attention to your disability; instead, focus your resume on convincing the potential employer you have the skills, qualifications and experience to perform well in the role.

- ✔ If your disability is visible, avoid providing any details until the interview has been set in concrete. Once the interview is confirmed with the recruiter, mention casually in your conversation any other specific requirements you may have including venue and wheelchair access, parking requirements and other special need provisions.

- ✔ If your disability is not visible (such as a mental illness or epilepsy), don't delve into your condition unless you have specific requirements that need to be catered for during the interview.

- ✔ Be discrete about any special equipment you may require in the future to perform your job efficiently, even if the items are inexpensive or you're willing to purchase them yourself. Win the interview first. Reasonable accommodation issues are best brought up when everything is pretty much in the bag.

- ✔ Do some research to find out what assistance and support services are available to you. For example, if you're deaf or have a hearing impairment you may be able to access the services of an Auslan interpreter.

For those in Australia, you can find more information on disabilities and employment from the Australian government's JobAccess site at www.jobaccess.gov.au, as well as specialist websites such as:

- ✔ **NOVA Employment:** (www.novaemployment.com.au)

- ✔ **Disability Employment Australia:** (www.disabilityemployment.org.au)

For those in New Zealand, check out the government website
www.careers.govt.nz, as well as specialist sites of interest,
such as:

- ✔ **The Association for Supported Employment in New Zealand:** (www.asenz.org.nz)
- ✔ **Workbridge:** (www.workbridge.co.nz)

Divulging your gender

Like it or lump it, gender discrimination does exist. The *Sex
Discrimination Act 1984* in Australia and the *Human Rights
Act 1993* in New Zealand offer you the right to take action if
treated unfairly on the basis of sex, marital status or pregnancy.
However, most employers that discriminate don't come out and
tell you why you didn't get the job. Sadly, too many employers
will still skirt the law and wipe your job chances based on your
gender.

The best approach to avoid gender discrimination is to never list
the following personal details in your resume:

- ✔ Gender
- ✔ Marital status
- ✔ Number and ages of children
- ✔ Notification of pregnancy

This information is irrelevant, so don't give the employer or
recruiter any reason to discriminate against you.

Chapter 6

Polishing to Perfection

· ·

In This Chapter

▶ Getting the content right

▶ Making sure your resume is legible

▶ Giving your resume a final once-over

▶ Running through your checklist

· ·

So long, farewell . . . you've pulled together a wonderful resume and now you just can't wait to send it off and get that job. Hang on a minute! Have you checked, double-checked and triple-checked your resume? Part and parcel of sending off a job application is doing a final check — looking carefully at the content and presentation, and going through your resume with a fine-tooth comb. Don't be too hasty and spoil your job chances by submitting an unprofessional document that's hard to read or contains errors.

In this chapter, we talk about ways you can make a recruiter's or hiring manager's job easier by paying attention to a few finer details, and how to present your job application in a design sense and in terms of the electronic format. We finish with a checklist that covers everything you need to know to polish your resume to perfection.

Going the Extra Mile Pays Off

You can make life easy for recruiters and hiring managers by paying careful attention to the content of your resume. Stay in their good books by taking note of these four tricks that may just put you above the rest of the herd.

Customising your resume to the job

Before you send off your job application, check to see you have customised your resume specifically to the role. Jog your memory about the position by reading through the job ad, and highlighting the skills, competencies and personal attributes required to do the job. From the highlighted list, figure out what skills you have and incorporate these into a career profile (or career summary), which is a summary of your relevant work history that you should place at the top of your resume. We describe the career profile in detail in Chapter 3. In the main body of your resume, focus greatest attention on the responsibilities and achievements from your career history that are of greatest relevance to the job you are applying for. For those jobs of least relevance, just list the position, the company and dates of employment.

Spice up your resume with optional extras if they relate to the role you're applying for. For example, you may want to mention any professional memberships that are relevant to the position. (For more information on the different elements you can add to flavour your resume, refer to Chapter 3.)

Documenting dialling codes

If you've just come back from working your way around the world, include international dialling codes in your resume, particularly if you're listing overseas referees. Including the codes saves recruiters lots of time when contacting past employers.

Here is an example of how to list overseas referees in your resume:

David Shepherd

Business Development Manager

Kiwi Connections (Auckland, New Zealand)

(p) 0011 64 9 300 3000

(f) 0011 64 9 300 3001

(e) d.shepherd@kiwiconnections.co.nz

Table 6-1 lists the international country codes for some popular working destinations. Note that the international code is 0011 when dialling from Australia, and 00 when dialling from New Zealand. For example, if you are a candidate in Australia listing a referee in the UK, the full dialling code would be 0011 44 followed by the UK area code and the local phone number.

Table 6-1	International Dialling Codes
Country	*Numbers to List*
Australia	61 + area code + local phone number
Canada	1 + area code + local phone number
China	86 + area code + local phone number
Hong Kong	852 + area code + local phone number
India	91 + area code + local phone number
Ireland	353 + area code + local phone number
Japan	81 + area code + local phone number
New Zealand	64 + area code + local phone number
Papua New Guinea	675 + area code + local phone number
United Kingdom	44 + area code + local phone number
United States of America	1 + area code + local phone number

Always list fax and email details, plus landline and mobile phone numbers, for overseas referees if you can. Some employers will reference check via email instead of phoning the other side of the world. Many reference checkers will only use a landline, not a mobile phone number, so they can first go through a company reception to verify the manager's title. By providing all points of contact you're well and truly covered.

Briefing your referees

You need to make checking your references as smooth as possible for recruiters and employers. They don't want to waste time calling people who don't remember you or spend time chasing up contact phone numbers. These pointers will keep your referees in check and make life easier for recruiters:

- ✔ **Always request permission.** Be polite and ask permission before you put a person down as your referee. Most people don't like to receive unexpected calls — give referees the chance to think about what they'll say about your work performance.

- ✔ **Brief referees on the roles you're applying for.** No-one likes being put on the spot — brief your referees on the sort of positions you're going for, the key skills and qualifications being sought and even some highlights from your shared work history. Keep your referees updated on your progress and always send your thanks in appreciation of the time and effort your referees have provided on your behalf.

- ✔ **Track down your referee's current details.** If it's been a long time since you've been in touch, check their contact and work details. You want to provide the correct phone numbers and a current job title for each referee you provide. This saves recruiters time and effort locating the whereabouts of missing people. Trust me, they'll love you for it!

- ✔ **Be careful who you list.** Don't let your referees wreck your job chances. If you're unsure of what they're going to say, ask them. Better to be safe than sorry. If you have an inkling your referee may be vindictive and negative, don't use that person. Try to think of other work-related referees who have supervised you at work, and can comment objectively on your performance. We give you more information about referees in Chapter 3.

Localising the language

The language you use in your resume needs to be simple, clear and easy-to-understand. Bear the following in mind when choosing the right words to use:

- ✔ **Spell out acronyms.** Sure, you may know BDD means Business Development Division, but don't assume everyone else does. Spell out acronyms, particularly if they're jargon used only at your last place of work.

- ✔ **Get rid of the military talk.** Attention! If you're planning to march your way straight into a non-military role, you may need to translate your army, navy or air force lingo into plain English for recruiters.

✔ **Thumbs up for industry jargon**. Some recruiters search for prospective candidates in their database using keywords. Ensure you're not overlooked by filling your resume with common industry jargon. Refer to Chapters 3 and 4 for more on keywords.

✔ **Be positive**. Don't turn the recruiter off by using negative language. Words like 'fired', 'sacked' and 'poor performance' don't belong in a resume.

✔ **Use active voice**. Talk in an active rather than a passive voice. When you write in an active voice the person performs the action, instead of the action being performed on the person (passive voice). 'Developed a TV advertising campaign' is more powerful than 'A TV advertising campaign was developed by me'.

✔ **Watch your language**. Steer clear of language that is overly aggressive, boastful or fluffy. Use specific rather than general wording. Talk it up by using positive, energetic language that communicates who you are, what you've achieved and what you're looking for.

Perfecting the Presentation

Your resume needs to look attractive and be legible. A good design that uses easy-to-read fonts and presents your information clearly can impress recruiters, but before recruiters can lay eyes on your masterpiece they need to be able to open it. Do a last-minute design check and then, if you're sending your resume by email, make sure it's produced in a common file format that is certain to open easily, such as Word.

Keeping it stylish and legible

Before you say goodbye to your resume, check that you haven't used more than one or two fonts, and that your fonts aren't too flowery, elaborate or hard to read. Fonts that are easy on the eye include Arial, Times New Roman, Calibri, Verdana or Tahoma. Don't go overboard with italics — use bold for headings. Keep your font size large enough to read but not so big it makes the resume too long.

Avoid using colour schemes that look overdone and make the text difficult to decipher. Recruitment consultants often shortlist on screen rather than reviewing printed documents, so choose shades that are tasteful and don't mix colours. Unless you're applying for a design role, keep it simple with black text on a white background.

Cramming too much into your resume makes it difficult to read. Make sure you use plenty of bullet points, particularly for your responsibilities and achievements. A good amount of white space makes it easier on the eye.

Using standard software

Steer clear of whipping up documents in obscure word processing programs. You're better off sticking to conventional Microsoft Office programs, namely Word.

A PDF format is an option, but not everyone welcomes a PDF. A recruiter may wish to re-format your skills and qualifications to present them in an in-house format, so will find Word easier to edit.

Including any certifications or added information requested by the recruiter requires you to provide extra attachments when you're emailing your resume. Ensure your name and contact details are on every page of every document you send in case the pages get separated at any point after you have sent off your application. Before you send your job application to a recruiter, make sure all your attachments will open properly at the other end.

Here are a few handy hints to keep in mind before attaching and sending your resume:

- ✔ **Email yourself.** Sneak a preview of your resume before submitting it to employers by emailing yourself the files — check that the formatting is correct on-screen.

- ✔ **Send to a friend.** Do a test run to see how the files transmit by emailing your resume to a friend and asking him or her to read over the finished product.

- ✔ **Don't rush.** Try not to apply for jobs when you're in a hurry. You're more likely to do silly things such as sending emails to the wrong person. Don't forget to add any attachments when you send your resume by email. Forgetting the attachment is so easy to do but makes you look unprofessional.

Doing a Final Check

Do a final *final* check before sending off. Even better, ask a trusted friend or family member to proof your documents for you. Following are a few tips on what to look for when finalising your document and a checklist you or a friend can use to make sure you've covered everything. Make sure your resume

✓ **Contains your contact details**. Don't sabotage your job opportunities by forgetting to include contact details in your resume. Recruiters are clever but they aren't psychic. Always include your current phone and mobile numbers, and email address on the first page.

✓ **Lists specific job duties**. Are your responsibilities clear and succinct? Do they mention what you were individually accountable for? Check to see you've used present tense for current roles and past tense for previous roles. (Refer to Chapter 3 to find out more about job responsibilities.)

✓ **Shows you're a go-getter**. Have you demonstrated your star qualities by listing achievements in your resume? Highlight the fact you're a dynamo by showcasing what you've accomplished in the past. How to present achievements is covered in more detail in Chapter 3.

✓ **Looks attractive**. Does your resume look attractive on the page and is it easy to read? Nothing is worse than a resume that's messy and difficult to follow. Don't make it too tizzy. A simple, clean design looks professional and makes a good first impression on the reader.

✓ **Uses consistent formatting**. Is your text formatted consistently from beginning to end? Check that any fonts and font sizes are uniform and spacing between text is exactly the same. Remember, if one heading is bold, all headings should be bold; if you use capital letters for job titles, keep it consistent for all positions.

Proofreading and more proofreading

Nothing bugs an employer more than a document full of errors. Typos and spelling mistakes stand out like a sore thumb and cast a shadow over your attention to detail and professionalism.

Even if you're a top-class speller who won the sixth-grade spellathon, you still need to check your work for typos and errors. It's easy to slip up and miss the odd blooper or two if you're not careful. A good plan to follow before you send your resume away is to

✔ Run a spellcheck on the document. However, beware that a spell checker could be programmed to Americanised spellings so check this and change any words to Australian or New Zealand English as you go along.

✔ Print and read the document out loud, spotting the mistakes as you go.

✔ Look through your work a second time — reading the text word for word. Watch out for simple mistakes like commas being used instead of full stops, two spaces being used instead of one, and 'there' being replaced for 'their'.

✔ Safeguard yourself by asking a friend, flatmate, partner or family member to proofread for errors.

Resume Checklist

Use this handy checklist to make sure your resume is recruiter-ready. Go through and tick off each item once completed.

Tailoring your resume to the job

☐ Research the organisation

☐ Read through the job description/job ad

☐ Customise to the job

☐ Include relevant responsibilities and achievements

Content

Contact details

- ☐ Name (use slightly larger font and bold typeface so it stands out)
- ☐ Current address
- ☐ Phone number/s (home, work, mobile)
- ☐ Email address
- ☐ URL to your website, work-related blog or social media profile, if applicable
- ☐ Do not include marital status, date of birth, age, race, religion, gender, salary details

Educational qualifications

- ☐ Most recent qualifications listed first
- ☐ University qualifications listed before certificate, diploma and other professional development courses
- ☐ Names of qualifications in full
- ☐ Majors, minors and other specialisations listed
- ☐ Institution awarding qualification listed/campus
- ☐ Year completed
- ☐ Academic achievements, special awards, prizes, honours, scholarships (if applicable)

High school details (for school leavers and graduates only)

- ☐ Secondary school/location
- ☐ Name of qualification
- ☐ Year completed
- ☐ University entrance score (for example, HSC, OP, TER, UAI)
- ☐ Academic achievements, special awards, prizes, scholarships (if applicable)

Work experience

☐ Highlight full-time, part-time, volunteer, vacation clerkships, internships, work experience

☐ Most recent position listed first

☐ Job titles listed

☐ Company names in full/location

☐ Company descriptions (if organisation is unknown)

☐ Dates of employment (months and years are preferable)

☐ Responsibilities

☐ Achievements

Referees

☐ Request permission beforehand

☐ Jot down two or three work-related referees (preferably direct supervisors or managers)

☐ Use recent referees

☐ If you were self-employed or in a partnership, put down suppliers, customers, business partners or other key contacts as referees

☐ Check to see your referees' contact details are current

☐ Do not list character referees or attach references (unless requested)

☐ Give referees a copy of the job description and selection criteria (public sector positions)

☐ Names of referees

☐ Job titles (for example, Relationship Manager, Team Leader)

☐ Company

☐ Phone number/mobile

☐ Email address (if applicable)

☐ Include international dialling codes and fax numbers for overseas referees

☐ If your referees have moved on to other jobs, put down their current title and company followed by a statement substantiating the relationship — for example, Former Accountant at Walker and Co.

Optional

- ☐ Career objectives
- ☐ Extracurricular activities
- ☐ Interests
- ☐ Key skills
- ☐ IT/computer skills (hardware, software programs, versions used, level of proficiency)
- ☐ Languages
- ☐ Professional memberships

Presentation/layout

- ☐ Professional and attractive, clean and crisp
- ☐ Shows individuality/personality
- ☐ Well laid out, concise and easy to read
- ☐ Used a plain, clear font — for example, Times New Roman, Arial, Calibri, Verdana or Tahoma
- ☐ Font size is between 10 and 12 points (main text)
- ☐ Only one or two fonts used, in black
- ☐ Bullet points used to break up large chunks of text
- ☐ Plenty of white space
- ☐ Standard margins — 2 to 2.5 centimetres (0.75 to 1 inch)
- ☐ Consistent layout
- ☐ Pages are numbered. Name is included on every page.
- ☐ Printed on white or off-white paper (if sending hard copy)
- ☐ Printed on a quality laser/ink-jet printer (if sending hard copy)
- ☐ Resume is no more than 2 to 4 pages long

Writing style/language

- ☐ Commenced sentences with action verbs (past tense for previous positions, present tense for current jobs)
- ☐ Included industry specific keywords

☐ Used an active rather than a passive voice

☐ Logical and sequential flow

☐ Used short, succinct sentences

☐ Spelt out acronyms in full; no slang or abbreviations

☐ Spellchecked and proofread

Sending it off

☐ Forward your resume to the appropriate person or email address

☐ Send in the format requested, such as post, fax, email

☐ Send in the file format requested (Word, PDF)

☐ Submit on time

Part III

Resume Relatives

WrapStarz relaunch brochure • Tri-fold • 4 colour process • 150GSM gloss

Brochure Design www.tjrankin.com.au timothyjamesrankin digital designer

Visit www.dummies.com/extras/writingresumes coverlettersau for a (free!) article about resume relatives.

In this part...

- ✔ Craft a successful cover letter: Create a compelling introduction, body and conclusion.

- ✔ Develop an energised social media profile to support your resume and get you noticed for the right reasons.

- ✔ Prepare application forms and collate supporting documents for your applications.

Chapter 7

Writing a Winning Cover Letter

. . . .

In This Chapter

▶ Discovering the purpose of the cover letter

▶ Examining the parts of a cover letter

▶ Presenting some cover letter examples

▶ Avoiding the hazards of cover letter writing

. . . .

*Y*ou have identified a great job and know you can perform well in the role. Now all you have to do is convey that message up-front and with confidence to your prospective employer. Get the employer hooked right from the word go with a spot-on cover letter that introduces who you are and why you're the best person for the job. A well-written, personalised cover letter also increases the chances that your resume will be thoroughly read.

Your cover letter serves as an at-a-glance insight into why you're a good fit for the role on offer. With this summary of your brilliant career you can stun a recruiter with the quality and relevance of your skills, qualifications, knowledge and experience. In today's competitive job market, your cover letter needs to draw attention fast; it gives you the chance to show off the fact that you've done your homework. You're not applying for *a* job, you're applying for *the* job — the job that is perfect for you.

This chapter introduces the cover letter, shows you the essential elements and layout, and provides some examples of different cover letters to fit your needs. We also share some practical hints and tips to help you design a powerful letter that will give you that winning edge over your competition.

A Handshake in Words

Most employers these days still require a cover letter. A well-written cover letter establishes you as a serious contender for the job in only a few paragraphs. It shows you're not just applying for anything and everything you see; you've assessed the criteria spelled out in the job ad and now you're introducing yourself as shortlist material.

A cover letter is like the introductory handshake at an interview. It's a personal greeting on paper or (more likely these days) in an email that breaks the ice and introduces you to the prospective employer. It outlines why you're making contact and why you'd be a valuable employee.

'I' statements work well to express how you fit the bill — just don't overuse them. See the example cover letters later in this chapter (in the section 'Identifying the Right Cover Letter Type for Your Needs') for inspiration.

Your cover letter serves a number of purposes. It can act as

- ✔ **A letter of introduction**. Give the employer a snapshot of who you are by introducing yourself in the cover letter. Tell the recruiter why you're writing and how you fit the bill. When writing to an employer, you can add a line about why you want to work for their particular organisation.

- ✔ **A selling mechanism**. You only have 30 seconds to grab a recruiter's attention so don't be shy. The cover letter is your first opportunity to sell your skills, abilities, qualifications and work experience.

- ✔ **The entrée before the main meal**. A strong cover letter jumps out at the recruiter or employer and sparks interest. It whets the appetite and arouses interest in your resume before it has even been read.

- ✔ **An example of your writing skills**. Your cover letter gives the recruiter or employer a feel for your written communication skills. It demonstrates your ability to construct a letter, convey well thought-out ideas and shows off your wonderful eye for detail.

- ✔ **A perfect skills match**. A well-crafted cover letter is customised to the job and the employer. It's not a generic 'one size fits all' letter you send to a large number of employers. Your cover letter spells out how your skills match perfectly to the requirements of the role. Figure 7-3, later in this chapter, provides an example of a cover letter tailored to a job ad.

Initiative scores highly on a recruiter's checklist, so before you start putting together your cover letter, take the trouble to do some research on the company and job. If the specific employer is not mentioned in a job ad posted by a recruitment agency, do your homework on the industry sector. Look for telltale clues as to who the employer could be through phrases in the job ad such as 'market leader', 'leading multinational company' or 'family-owned business'. If the company name is on the job ad, use its website to find information on the company's products and services, corporate culture and values. By going to this trouble, the recruiter will know you're genuinely interested in the role.

Anatomy of a Cover Letter

After you've done your homework and gathered all the research you need, you're ready to start writing. In this section, we show you the essential elements of a cover letter. A cover letter has three main parts:

- ✔ **Introduction**. This includes the contact details and addresses, salutation and a subject line if appropriate, and the first paragraph of your letter. This opening paragraph contains a brief statement telling the reader why you're making contact.

- ✔ **Body**. This is where you dazzle the reader by rattling off your skills, abilities, qualifications, experience and achievements. Highlight why you want to work for the firm and how you can meet the company's needs. Hold the recruiter's attention by showing off how your experience and skills match closely to the recruitment criteria for the job.

- ✔ **Conclusion**. This outlines the next step of the process and confirms your availability. Don't forget to mention your telephone number so that an employer can reach you to arrange an interview time.

Figure 7-1 shows the format for a cover letter, so you can see how these elements are used.

[Your name]

[Address]

[Suburb] [State] [Postcode]

[Telephone number/mobile]

[Email address]

[Current date]

[Contact person's name]

[Title]

[Company name/Department]

[Address]

[Suburb] [State] [Postcode]

Dear Mr, Ms, Miss [Surname]

RE: [Job Title] [Ref: xxxxxxx]

Introduction

In the opening paragraph, outline the main reason for establishing contact. Are you responding to an advertised vacancy? If so, where and when was the job advertised? Are you cold-calling and looking for job openings? Have you been referred by a contact?

Body

The second and third paragraphs are the body of your cover letter. Tell the recruiter what skills, knowledge, experience, qualifications and personal attributes you can bring to the role. Why are you the best person for the job? What are your selling points? Showcase a few achievements that you're particularly proud of. Outline why you're interested in working for the company and highlight how you can contribute to the company's success. Remember to tailor your cover letter to the job.

Conclusion

In the final paragraph, confirm your availability. Outline the next steps of the process. Don't forget to include your contact details, so an employer can reach you to arrange an interview.

Yours sincerely

(Include your signature here)
No signature required if sending the cover letter electronically

[Type your name]

Enc.

Figure 7-1: The essential elements of a traditional cover letter.

We explore these parts in more detail in the following sections.

Making an introduction

Ensure you start your cover letter with the following essential information.

Your contact details

You can create your cover letter as a separate document or write it in the body of an email message. If you choose to place your cover letter in the body of an email, include your phone number. When creating a separate document, include your name, mobile or landline number and email address. Including your postal address is optional.

Date

If creating a separate document, type the current date at the left margin, using the day, month and year, like this: 17 January 2014. Don't write the date on an email cover letter. The date will automatically appear on the email.

Contact's name and address

Make sure you address your cover letter to the right person, and use his or her correct title. If no name is given in the job ad, ring the organisation and find out the key contact's name — don't automatically send it to the HR manager or managing director of the company (they may not be the best person). Also, check the correct spelling of both the person's name and that of the company. Including the address of the employer in an email cover letter is optional.

We don't recommend mass mailing or emailing cover letters to hundreds of firms in your industry. Sooner or later, you're bound to accidentally address your cover letter to Mrs Taylor instead of Mr Adams, or call the organisation by its competitor's name. The trick is to be selective in the jobs you apply for. How could you truly be qualified for hundreds of roles? Tailor a cover letter to your selected organisation and proofread everything prior to sending. Better yet, get a second pair of eyes to proofread your efforts.

Salutation

If possible, use the appropriate person's name, instead of addressing him or her as 'Dear Sir/Madam' or opening with 'To whom it may concern'. Adding that little personal touch shows recruiters you've used your initiative.

Don't get too chummy with employers — avoid starting your cover letter with first names, such as 'Dear Bob', a sore spot for some recruiters. Instead, stick to surnames (Dear Mr Kiri) in the salutation unless you're on a first-name basis with the recruiter.

If the recruiter is female and you're unsure of her marital status, don't guess and write 'Mrs' or 'Miss'. When in doubt, use 'Ms'.

Subject line

If you're responding to a specific ad, include the job title in the *subject line* of the cover letter or in the email's 'Subject' field, and quote the reference or job number (if one is mentioned), like this:

RE: Marketing Assistant role (Ref No MA3456/07)

A reference number is simply a code that employers use to distinguish one job from another. Some companies advertise different jobs at the same time, so make the recruiter's life easier by stating the job and the reference number in your cover letter. For government jobs, look for the vacancy reference number or job number contained in the job description or take a peek at the ad posted on the public sector job board.

For cold-call or speculative cover letters, use the subject line of the email to grab attention. Write a short, specific message that encourages the recruiter to open and read your email.

Employers often decide whether to delete or open emails by reading the subject line. Never leave the subject line blank. By doing so, they may accidentally discard your email or leave it unopened in their inbox.

Opening paragraph

In the opening paragraph, outline the main reason for establishing contact. Are you responding to an advertised vacancy? If so, where and when was the job advertised? Are you cold-calling and looking for job openings? Have you been referred by a contact?

If you were recommended by a colleague, manager or your best buddy, make sure you name-drop in your cover letter, particularly if your contact is well respected and liked in the industry. Many jobs these days are filled through personal referral. Some employers even pay their employees a fee if they introduce a candidate who then lands the job.

Building the body

The body of your cover letter needs to be only two or three paragraphs long. Concise but still detailed, it explains to the recruiter or employer what skills, knowledge, experience, qualifications and personal attributes you can bring to the specific role on offer. Why are you the best person for the job? What are your selling points? Showcase a few achievements that you're particularly proud of that relate to the role.

Reasons for pitching for the job

Sell your strongest points tailored to the job on offer. Show exactly how your skills and experience match the criteria for the job. To pull it off, firstly you need to find out what's required to do the job. Read the job ad closely and underline the key criteria. Most ads list what the successful candidate must have. Next, think about what skills, qualifications, knowledge and experience you have that relates to the criteria, and incorporate this into the body of your cover letter. Add a bit of your own personality into your cover letter for extra sparkle.

Reasons for joining the company

Make a connection with the recruiter straightaway by indicating your reasons for wanting to join the firm. Think about the company and what makes it stand out. Aspects you could mention are the firm's reputation, client base, culture, development opportunities and work challenges offered. If you've done your research, this sentence is a cinch.

Highlight your career achievements

Demonstrate why the employer would be mad not to take you on board by including a couple of your top achievements relevant to the job. Including relevant achievements shows off the sort of energy and drive you will bring to the job if hired. Refer to Chapter 3 for more on highlighting your achievements.

Conclusion

In the final paragraph, end on a positive note by suggesting a face-to-face meeting or a Skype meeting if you live interstate or overseas. The conclusion wraps up the letter and outlines your next action.

Outlining the next steps of the process

If you have not already done so in the body of your cover letter, use the closing paragraph to mention that your resume is attached. You can also thank the recruiter or employer for considering your application and clarify the next step of the process. For example, be blunt but polite and make reference to the likelihood of an interview — indicate when you're available and that you'd love the opportunity to discuss the position further. If you're writing a speculative cover letter, you may want to end by stating you will follow up with a phone call or an email within the week.

Ensuring you're contactable

Make sure you put down a contact number in your closing statement, so an employer can reach you to arrange an interview.

Signing off

Sign off your cover letter with 'Yours sincerely' or 'Yours faithfully'. Use 'Yours sincerely' if you have addressed the letter to a particular person; use 'Yours faithfully' if you don't have a contact name. Type your name on a line at the bottom but leave space for your signature if you're sending a hard copy of the cover letter. For cover letters sent by email or posted online, just add your name. Also triple-check that your resume is attached to the email or included in the online application.

Never promise something in your cover letter you can't deliver. If you mention in the closing paragraph that you plan to follow up by phone or email at the end of a week, diarise the date and do it.

Identifying the Right Cover Letter Type for Your Needs

Cover letters come in different styles or formats, depending on how you're approaching the employment opportunity. The three main types are:

- ✔ **Cover letter in response to a job ad.** This type of cover letter is by far the most common and is written in response to a specific job advertisement. See Figures 7-2 and 7-3 for an example ad and cover letter in response.

- ✔ **Referral cover letter.** This type of cover letter is written to an employer on the recommendation of a personal contact. The person who referred you to the organisation is mentioned in the first paragraph of the cover letter. See Figure 7-4 for an example.

  Always get the okay first before using the name of one of your contacts in a cover letter. A personal introduction to a recruitment consultant or hiring manager is a great way to stand out from the candidate pack. Employers in particular welcome such introductions as they believe their employees understand their culture and requirements and only refer candidates suited to their environment. Many even pay employees for referring candidates who are then hired.

- ✔ **Cold-call or unsolicited cover letter.** This type of cover letter is sent to an employer you would like to work for requesting a meeting or to be told if any *potential* vacancies arise within an organisation. See Figure 7-5 for an example.

First, review the job ad shown in Figure 7-2 carefully.

MANAGEMENT ACCOUNTANT

- **Market Leader – Global Manufacturer**
- **Focus on Analytical Review & Business Support**
- **Package Circa $130K/Sydney**

This is an opportunity for a Management Accountant to join this successful division of a high profile and profitable multinational. In Australia, the business has an annual turnover of $90M and is recognised as the market leader in their sector.

The position of Management Accountant will report to the Head Office Financial Controller and is responsible for:

- Compilation of financial forecasts to reflect any changes in operating conditions.
- Development and initiation of policies and procedures to enhance reporting processes.
- Variance analysis, including reporting on cost irregularities to management.
- Production of management reports for Senior Management.

You will be a qualified Accountant, with exposure to large integrated manufacturing systems, have a high level of self-motivation and the ability to work autonomously. The role requires an individual with broad commercial skills who can add value to senior management's ability to analyse and predict business performance.

Please apply online via www.financerecruitment.com.au and quote Ref. No 2B/03009. Enquiries can be made to **Lisa Hamilton at Finance Recruitment** on (02) 8233 2222.

Figure 7-2: An advertised job.

Use a highlighter pen to pick out all the salient points you need to address in your cover letter. In our example, those details would include the need for the candidate to be a qualified accountant with experience in manufacturing as well as the ability to use software and other tools to analyse data and create business projections. Highlighting the name of the key contact in the job ad as well as the employer's website address and the job reference number is also important. On other ads, highlight the date applications close.

Julie Chan
5/4 Aster Avenue,
CHATSWOOD NSW 2067
0438 xxx xxx
Email: julie.chan@bigpond.com

21 February 2014

Ms Lisa Hamilton
Finance Recruitment
Level 2, 10 Smith St
SYDNEY NSW 2000

Dear Ms Hamilton

RE: MANAGEMENT ACCOUNTANT – 2B/03009

I read your advertisement for a Management Accountant posted on CareerOne.com.au
with great interest as I believe I have the experience and qualifications needed to
succeed in the role.

You will find my resume attached, but of particular relevance to the role is my
experience working in a contract role as a Management Accountant with BHP
Billington and the three years I spent in a similar role at Company X. I am also a
Chartered Accountant and an active member of the Institute of Chartered Accountants.

As you will see from my resume, I have led a project that created reporting processes
and policies for a new division of Company X. My work on this project was recognised
when I was named Staff Member of the Year in 2012.

I would welcome an opportunity to meet with you at an interview to discuss my
application further.

Yours sincerely

Julie Chan

Figure 7-3: Cover letter in response to the job ad in Figure 7-2.

Ben Harris
54 Jones Street,
ULTIMO NSW 2009
(02) 9727 3411
Email: bharris@email.com

Monday 18 March 2013

Mr Paul Mann
Chief Financial Officer
Doby Electronics and Systems
Level 12, 127 Archer Street
CHATSWOOD NSW 2067

Dear Mr Mann

RE: Senior Operations Manager

Your colleague Bill Wong and I used to work together at Phillips Electronics. Bill spotted the role of Senior Operations Manager at Doby Electronics and Systems on your intranet and sent me the job description, believing I would fit in well with the culture at Doby and that my skills and experience match what you are looking for to fill the role.

After reading the job description carefully, I see many areas where I could use my skills and qualifications to make a success of the role on offer. I have enclosed my resume for your perusal but would draw your attention to the following aspects of my work history:

- I am a CPA qualified accountant and possess a sound mix of financial, technical and commercial skills and experience.

- I joined the accounting team at Phillips Electronics five years ago and was promoted to Operations Manager three years ago, gaining valuable relevant experience in this time.

- At Phillips, I work with the ED team to prepare monthly management reports across all units of the business for the Board.

- As a key member of the Phillips Electronics quality systems team, I have been responsible for sourcing and introducing a range of new systems including for payroll and HR and procurement.

I would welcome an opportunity to meet with you at your convenience to discuss what I could contribute to the Senior Operations Manager role.

Yours sincerely

Ben Harris

Figure 7-4: A cover letter when you've been referred to a company or for a particular job.

Aimee Nairn
M: 0273 xxxxx
Email: aimee.nairn@telecom.co.nz

26 February, 2014

Ms Linda Krimstein
Account Director
Zoom Digital Agency
Level 4, 16 Wolfe Street
Auckland NZ

Dear Ms Krimstein

After reading the article in the *New Zealand Herald* about the launch of Zoom Digital Agency and your plans to build up the team, I write to introduce myself as a potential future team member.

I enclose my resume for your consideration, but of particular relevance is my four years working in the digital media space in both Melbourne and London in account management and business development.

Originally from Auckland, I recently returned home and would love to be part of the team working to make the Zoom Digital Agency a huge success in New Zealand.

I will follow up this email in a few days to see if there is a convenient time to drop by your office and chat about what I could contribute to Zoom.

Yours sincerely

Aimee Nairn

Figure 7-5: A cover letter when you're approaching an employer or recruiter 'cold' (there has been no job advertised).

Cover letters for casual and temporary roles

If you're hunting for casual or temp work, be sure to include the following in your cover letter:

✔ **Days and hours you can work.** If you're a student paying your way through university, or perhaps a backpacker touring Australia or New Zealand, remember that employers and recruitment agencies need to know when and how long you can work. State clearly your availability and whether you're interested in morning, afternoon, evening, weekend, full days or vacation work only.

✔ **Type of work you're seeking.** We know we may be stating the obvious but articulate the type of work you're searching for in your cover letter. Suppose you're scouting out jobs with an environmental non-profit organisation: State whether you're interested in working in the field of research, fundraising, training, supervising volunteers or general administrative tasks and so on.

Similarly, if you're searching for temporary office work through a recruitment agency, state clearly whether you're interested in all kinds of office administration positions—reception, secretarial, personal assistant, general office support or customer service—or whether you only want a certain type of administration assignment. After all, the recruiter won't know unless you tell them.

✔ **Preferred location.** Indicate your location preferences, particularly if you want to work for a large retail chain or a company with multiple offices or outlets. Don't forget to include why that office or location would be your top pick. Also, when you apply for jobs through a recruitment agency, put down whether you're interested in working in the central business district or in the suburbs. It's also helpful to mention whether or not you have your own transport.

Covering All Bases: Cover Letter Tips and Tricks

We have already covered a lot of ground, and your cover letter is probably looking the part now, but here are a few final thoughts to ensure your cover letter is a real winner.

Making it a one page wonder

Your cover letter should only be one page long. Any longer and you're giving too much information, taking up too much of a recruiter's or employer's time, and demonstrating that you can't summarise using a clear, concise writing style.

The recruiter or employer is time-poor, and sifting through applications for the job role you're after is just one of many tasks on their 'to-do' list.

Keeping it simple

Don't go over the top with the design of your cover letter: Keep it simple and easy to read. Use the same font and style as you use in your resume. Use plain fonts such as Arial, Times New Roman, Calibri, Verdana and Tahoma, because these ooze professionalism. Keep font sizes between 10 and 12 point (depending on the font). Steer clear of using graphics, fancy borders and never include a photo of yourself. Left-align your cover letter as well — this style suits current fashion and looks a lot neater.

Spacing is in

No-one likes reading mountains and mountains of straight text. Not only is this hard on the eyes, but it's also a little overwhelming to the reader. Use white space to give your cover letter a lift, and remember to increase space between paragraphs. Leave enough space for margins too, while remembering to keep your cover letter to one page.

Making style count

Your cover letter needs to be inviting to the reader. If you're sending your cover letter and resume by post, print it out on white paper. Keep in mind, however, that most job applications are sent by email these days, so be sure to keep the style of your email clean and easy to read as well.

Spellang mistakes—ooops!

Make sure that your cover letter is error free. Don't just rely on spellcheck, and beware of words that sound the same but are not the same, such as 'role' being misspelled as 'roll'—it drives recruiters crazy. Don't set off on the wrong foot by not proofreading your work thoroughly. Always take the time to read through your cover letter carefully before you shoot off your application to the employer. Better yet, ask a friend who's a good speller to proof it for you. Sometimes a fresh set of eyes can catch a mistake you've overlooked.

Using the right language

Be mindful of the language you use in your cover letter. Here are eight *don'ts* to bear in mind when it comes to language usage in your cover letter:

- ✔ **Don't be too pushy**. Being too aggressive and overpowering in your cover letter is an instant turn-off. Sure, sell your skills, qualifications and achievements with confidence but don't be intimidating.

- ✔ **Don't come across as a desperado**. You may have been trying to break into the job market for some time, but don't come across as desperate and willing to take any job that comes along. Apply for jobs you're genuinely interested in.

- ✔ **Don't use negative statements**. Making comments such as 'Although I don't have . . .' or 'Despite being . . .' does little to instil confidence in your abilities. Instead, put a positive spin on your sentences by using words such as 'I have . . .', 'I can . . .' or 'I am able to . . .'.

- ✔ **Don't waffle**. One of the big bugbears of recruiters is cover letters full of waffle. Don't beat around the bush, babbling on and on and on — get straight to the point. Write just one page of short, snappy statements. If you have the gift of the gab and can talk the hind legs off a donkey, edit your cover letter ruthlessly after you've written it.

- ✔ **Don't overuse the word 'I'**. Add a touch of variety to your cover letter by starting your paragraphs off in different ways.

✔ **Don't reveal too much.** Avoid pouring out your heart to the recruiter, particularly if you've experienced bad luck in the past. Sob stories are off putting.

✔ **Don't use too many big words.** Don't go overboard trying to impress the recruiter with your extensive vocabulary. Use simple, straightforward language and avoid using slang, colloquialisms or company acronyms.

✔ **Don't be fake.** Never ever lie, embellish the truth or pretend to be someone you're not in your cover letter. Any claims you make will be tested at job interview and again during the reference checking process.

Handwriting doesn't pay

Handwriting doesn't look professional and makes you look old-fashioned. If you don't have a computer at home, find one elsewhere. You can always access a computer at your local library and if you're not up to speed with your typing or computer skills, ask a friend or family member to help you.

Focusing on the employer

Too many people mention in a cover letter what they want from the employer, instead of focusing on the employer's needs. A well-written cover letter convinces the recruiter you have what it takes to do the job. It outlines why the company is special and talks about how you can add value to the company's business.

Keeping your salary a secret

Don't mention salary requirements in your cover letter. It may work against you. The second job interview or after a job offer is the best time to bring up money matters.

Email cover letter etiquette

Here are four do's to consider when emailing your cover letter to a prospective employer:

✔ Do keep your cover letter to one page.

✔ Do scan for viruses.

✔ Do send your cover letter and resume in the requested file format.

✔ Do check your spelling and grammar.

And now for the don'ts:

✔ Don't write your cover letter in all CAPITALS. This may give the impression you're shouting. Capital letters and italics are harder to read on screen.

✔ Don't use casual language. Cover letters are business documents.

✔ Don't use unprofessional-sounding email addresses.

✔ Don't use emoticons (such as :) to convey your mood), language short-cuts ('u' for 'you') or abbreviations ('thx' instead of 'thanks').

Chapter 8

Creating a Winning Social Media Profile

*S*ocial media is now as common a mode of communication as any other, and it's being used by everyone from prime ministers and government departments to everyday Australians and New Zealanders. Employers and recruiters also use social media in a range of ways, from promoting job ads via Twitter, LinkedIn and Facebook to screening potential new recruits. So, understanding social media and how it can help or hinder your chances of landing that dream job is pretty important.

Harnessing the power of social media as a career tool is something people of all ages and from all walks of life can do. Sometimes you hear people express the view that social media is only for the young or computer savvy. Keep in mind that whether you're a nurse, a licensed truck driver, a qualified tradesman, a teacher or a brick layer, you have already mastered a skill and qualification that has required more time and attention than creating a social media profile.

In this chapter, we explore the value of your social media profile and how it complements your resume. We also help you understand the importance of aligning your online profile to your personal brand (in other words, your professional reputation or the image you want to project to employers).

Finally, we take you through how to create a winning social media profile to boost your job-hunting prospects, and consider the importance of keeping your profile up to date.

Differentiating Your Social Media Profile from Your Resume

Think of your social media profile as a filtered version of your resume. It summarises your career and tells your story. It reflects your digital reputation, and is freely available to view (for more on managing who can view your social media profile, see the sidebar, 'Playing it safe online'). A traditional resume is more detailed, going into the specifics of your career history. Your resume is also carefully tailored for each role, whereas your social media profile provides an overview of who you are.

Your social media profile complements your resume, but isn't a substitute for it. You can't spot a job advertisement and then send an email with a link to your social media profile as a way of applying for the job. Employers and recruitment consultants will still want to see your resume when you're applying for a job, and your resume and cover letter need to be tailored to every job you go for.

Your social media profile offers potential employers a glimpse of how you choose to present yourself professionally to the world, and represents your *personal brand*, or reputation. We delve into developing and maintaining a professional personal brand in the next section and the later section 'Reviewing and Updating Your Personal Brand Online'.

Knowing What You Want Your Personal Brand to Stand for

Your *personal brand* is your reputation, or the words people use to describe you. Your personal brand is reliant on the actions you take that bring to life what people say about you, and is influenced by all your online activity, not just the activity on your professional profile pages. For more on managing your personal brand online, see the later section 'Reviewing and Updating Your Personal Brand Online'.

Your actions drive your personal brand, so ensure your online activity reflects the personal brand you want to project to potential employers. If you want your personal brand to say 'professional', don't use a holiday photo of yourself in beach gear for your social media profile picture. Likewise, if you want your personal brand to demonstrate that you're 'reliable', your social media profile shouldn't scream 'reckless' or 'casual' or anything that doesn't align with the image you want to project.

Your online actions are not the only thing that counts. If you want to be seen as professional, all your actions offline must reflect that reputation aspiration as well. Think through the other ways you project your professionalism. Punctuality, a polished personal presentation or even being known for turning in quality work on time all say 'professional'. And, if you're not all these things, it's never too late to start living up to your ideal personal brand!

When you decide to start job hunting, take the time to think about the qualities and attributes of most importance to the role you want. Do you possess these qualities and attributes? If not, what are you prepared to do to develop them?

Projecting your strengths

Your personal brand promotes your strengths to potential employers. Because you want your personal brand to reflect your strengths as you see them, take the time to list the qualities you want to convey to others when establishing your personal brand.

These could include

- ✔ Personal attributes, such as friendly, loyal, patient
- ✔ Professional attributes, such as diligent, reliable, technically minded
- ✔ Training and education, including certifications, degrees or trade or industry qualifications (in other words, well-qualified)

Take 10 minutes or so to list in each of the preceding areas three to five of your personal attributes that relate to the job you want (see Table 8-1). Start the exercise by writing the job title at the top of the page to help you list words that describe the ideal candidate for the job.

Table 8-1	Listing Your Strengths As You See Them

Job title: _____

_____

Personal attributes: _____

_____

Professional attributes: _____

_____

Training and education: _____

_____

By going through this exercise, you'll develop a clear picture of what you stand for. This awareness will help you to match your actions to the reputation you're keen to build. Another benefit of going through this exercise is understanding how much regard you have for your strengths and attributes. How your love of helping others drives your success in customer service, or how your powerful organisational skills make you a standout project manager quickly become clear. Completing this exercise is also helpful when you're creating your cover letter (refer to Chapter 7 for more on how to incorporate your strengths into your cover letter) or resume (refer to Chapter 3 for more on displaying your strengths in your resume).

Asking others for their views

You will be well served by also asking others (a colleague, peer or even a former manager) to share the words that come to mind when they think of you. Ask for both complimentary words and those that are less flattering, so you know where you can improve. Use Table 8-2 for this exercise.

Table 8-2	Listing What Others See As Your Strengths

Job title: _____

_____

Personal attributes: _____

_____

Professional attributes: _____

_____

Training and education: _____

_____

Reviewing and Updating Your Personal Brand Online

When starting the hunt for a new job, conduct an online audit of what is already out there about you before you create a new social media profile.

You might find yourself in old workplace photos or on the Facebook profile of a friend, tagged in photos or even videos. Comments you have made on blogs or forums may also be discoverable.

Old work photos and well thought-out comments are seldom harmful. However, party photos where you might be looking a bit too festive, photos that 'date' you, or angry or negative comments can harm you. Delete anything damaging, where possible.

Conducting a digital audit

Completing a digital audit offers you the chance to review your current online presence. If you think there might be something damning online, take action to minimise the damage. Be as thorough as possible, and use your audit to create a list of follow-up items.

Here are five steps we recommend you take:

1. **Type your name into a couple of different search engines such as Google and Bing to see what shows up.**

2. **Check to see how close to the top of the search results any positive items about you are.**

   You want the items that project you in the best possible light to be returned first.

3. **Conduct multiple searches, clicking on different tabs on the search engine including 'Web', 'Images' and even 'Videos' to cover all bases.**

4. **Search Facebook, but also type your name and then the word** Facebook **into a search engine to see what comes up.**

5. **Write down the URL (web address) of any page that includes information you would like to change.**

Changing what doesn't align to your brand

Keep a list of the words that describe your personal brand handy when conducting your online audit. Assess what you find against your list of positive words. Is what's out there a help or a hindrance? What would a recruitment consultant or an employer think if they came across the image or content you've found?

If you need to ask a friend or colleague to un-tag you from photos or delete a comment you have made, be polite. Requests will sound better than giving orders, especially if you explain why you need to spruce up your online image. If people understand you're searching for a job, they're far more likely to remove those funny photos from their birthday celebrations — even temporarily.

If you find unflattering photos of yourself on the website of an association or club you belong to, it could take a little longer to figure out the right person to approach. If the people you knew at the organisation in question have moved on, phone up and ask to speak to the web editor or the person responsible for updating the website or social media platform. Your best approach is to make a polite request for the material to be removed.

Sometimes, managing your online presence is out of your hands. If you can't remove something, prepare yourself for the possibility that you'll need to explain it one day.

Maybe you can't edit the past, but you can manage the future. Think about the personal brand you want to present when you're online, and try to align future online behaviour with this.

Knowing Who's Who in the Social Media Zoo

The social media space is dynamic and fast-moving, with new players coming into the market all the time. LinkedIn is the best-known social media platform for the career-minded but other social networks are out there too. Facebook, Google+ and Twitter are also used by those wanting to build their professional profile.

Before adopting a new social media platform, consider if the employers or recruiters you want to attract are using it. The ultra tech-savvy trendsetters in your peer group may have adopted a new platform, but it doesn't mean the gatekeepers to your dream job have heard of it.

In any social media, use the wizards (tools that guide you through the process), help centres and various tools on each platform to gain an in-depth understanding of what's on offer, and ask friends, family and contacts about their use of social media. What platforms do they prefer? What has worked best for them? How proficient are they in setting up profiles, loading photographs and attaching documents? Some people really enjoy playing around with online applications and ways to create content. See if anyone will volunteer to be your coach if you need help.

If you're looking for more information on the different social media platforms, the *For Dummies* series has a range of titles available, including *Social Networking For Dummies, Google+ For Dummies, Facebook For Dummies, Twitter For Dummies* and more (all published by Wiley).

The rise of social media

Research carried out in February 2013 by recruitment firm Robert Walters among 700 job hunters and 400 hiring managers in Australia and New Zealand demonstrates the increasing popularity of social media in the world of recruitment.

A high 74 per cent of those responding had a LinkedIn profile and 69 per cent had a Facebook profile. The research also found 62 per cent of the employers surveyed had used social media to check out a potential employee. Of these, 98 per cent used LinkedIn and 68 per cent Facebook. In 2011, research by an Australian telco found that only around 25 per cent of employers were checking out a candidate via social media. Wow, what a difference a few years make!

According to a report by research firm BRR Media, 61 per cent of Australia's largest listed companies had increased their use of social media in the year to July 2013. Of these, 58 per cent used social media primarily for recruitment, with LinkedIn the most popular platform used.

Linking up with LinkedIn

LinkedIn boasts a network of 225 million members worldwide, including more than four million users in Australia and over 800,000 in New Zealand. Creating a profile on LinkedIn is almost a must these days.

When you sign up on LinkedIn, you'll find an easy-to-follow wizard that helps you navigate the site, and plenty of help options once you're up and running. You can also connect with people and groups, search for jobs, link to examples of your work, recommend and endorse people and have them return the favour. And, recruitment consultants and employers looking for candidates with your particular skills can find your profile there as well. You can even see who has been viewing your profile and initiate contact with that person. People of all ages and professions use LinkedIn.

LinkedIn's strengths:

- ✔ LinkedIn is recognised as a social media platform for people promoting their professional strengths. It is not associated with a person's social life. LinkedIn is all about work.

✔ The platform is increasingly used by employers and recruiters to advertise jobs, headhunt new recruits and screen potential candidates.

✔ A LinkedIn profile boosts your professional profile, and the information is controlled by you so you can ensure your profile is full of positives. LinkedIn is also a great way to research potential employers and managers.

What to watch out for when using LinkedIn:

✔ If you're researching people on LinkedIn, they can tell you have been looking at them. It's a fine line between looking like a diligent researcher and looking like a stalker, so just be aware that when you view a person's profile, they can probably tell.

✔ Although you can indicate to the world that you're open to job offers, if your current boss sees your profile, awkward questions could follow.

✔ To make the most of LinkedIn and have a profile that attracts attention, you need to put in time and effort. Linking to examples of your work, attracting endorsements for your skills, asking others to provide written recommendations, joining groups and taking part in online discussions are all great ways to get noticed.

✔ You can set up a profile for free, but you'll need to pay a fee to access a range of more sophisticated features. This fee ranges, depending on the type and number of features you wish to access.

✔ Fee payers can also access a feature that enables them to view the profiles of others anonymously.

We explore creating a LinkedIn profile in more detail in the later section, 'Creating the Perfect Social Media Profile'.

Tweeting with Twitter

Twitter is not an exclusively professional social media network but many people use it as a way of building their personal brand. Users create a profile and then send out 'tweets' or messages of up to 140 characters. Prime ministers and presidents, company CEOs and leaders in every field now use Twitter so it's definitely not confined to one age group or type of profession. To use Twitter, all you do is set up a short profile. You can then follow other people on Twitter and hope they follow you.

Twitter's strengths:

✔ You don't have to use Twitter to broadcast tweets. Instead, you can set up a profile to follow industry leaders in your field, helping you to keep on top of developments in your industry.

✔ You can use Twitter to let people know that you have created a new resume, and direct them to where they can view it.

✔ You can interact with people in your industry who you may have never had the chance to meet in person.

✔ You can look out for new job opportunities. Twitter is increasingly used by employers and recruiters to alert potential candidates to new job postings.

What to watch out for when using Twitter:

✔ You can easily get steamed by a comment you read and want to retaliate with a zinger reply. However, if you want to use Twitter to promote the professional you, restraint is important.

✔ If you're employed and tweet that you have posted your resume, your employer may find out you're on the hunt for a new job.

✔ Twitter has been used to send computer viruses, so if a message — even from a trusted source — looks odd, delete it.

✔ Using Twitter to create and send tweets from your hand-held device can drive up your mobile bills (also true for any social media platform with an easy-to-use app). Take it easy.

Fathoming Facebook

Facebook first launched in 2004 and now has more than a billion users worldwide. You create a personal profile with a photo, post updates about your life, list the things you like, indicate the causes you follow, and share other personal information with people you 'friend', or connect with.

According to advertising firm Adcorp, more than 50 per cent of Australians and New Zealanders were active Facebook users in January 2013. However, both countries had seen a drop in usage and many social media commentators predict that Facebook will continue to lose users in favour of rising new networks such as Instagram, a photo and video sharing platform, and other international evolving social media sites. Facebook also poses a dilemma for most job hunters: Do you use the site as a career-related tool and censor yourself, or do you keep your profile for private use with your family and friends (by applying the maximum privacy settings to keep recruiters and employers out)? Many stories have hit the headlines the world over concerning people losing their jobs because of a rogue Facebook post.

If you're sharing your life publicly on a social networking site such as Facebook, be careful not to make derogatory remarks about previous employers or bosses. Remember your reputation is at stake, so always keep your personal profile professional.

Facebook's strengths:

- ✔ You can use Facebook to let your personal network know you're looking for a job. If you use Facebook for personal friends only, this is even more effective as friends are usually more willing to pass on any job leads they hear about, or even to introduce you to a hiring manager at their workplace.

- ✔ Many companies are now creating their own profiles and using these to post jobs, making Facebook an extra resource for finding the next great opportunity.

- ✔ You can 'friend' companies you want to work for and be in the front row when they post new jobs.

- ✔ Facebook is free to use and can help you connect with people you have not worked with or seen for many years. 'Friending' someone you went to school with, or worked with 10 years ago, is not considered socially strange.

What to watch out for when using Facebook:

- ✔ Employers are using Facebook as a screening tool to see the unguarded you. Ensure you apply maximum security settings.

- ✔ What an employer finds on your Facebook page is out of context because they don't know you. For example, say you like a certain rap song and connect to it through your Facebook account without having listened closely to the lyrics that happen to be pretty 'colourful' . . . An employer could easily get the wrong idea about you.

✔ Many people befriend their colleagues, including their manager. We don't recommend this. Too often, people forget who they've connected to and their comments about work filter back to their employer, landing them in hot water. Connecting to work colleagues is also awkward if you're reaching out to your network to help you look for a new job.

Getting to grips with Google+

Google+ claims to be the second-largest social networking site in the world, having surpassed Twitter in January 2013 (Facebook is still the largest). At the time of writing, Google+ had more than 350 million active users worldwide. Operated by Google Inc., it allows people to create a social and professional profile in a single place.

You don't 'friend' people like you do on Facebook; instead, you 'circle' them. Circles allow you to share different parts of your profile with different people. You also circle people you want to follow, and use circles to control what information goes where on your profile and who sees what. Google+ also offers additional features useful to the career-minded, such as a news feed of your updates (known as 'streams') and a communication tool called Hang Outs that allows for text- and video-based chat.

Strengths of Google+:

✔ You can create a single profile for both social and professional purposes.

✔ You get to pick and choose which parts of your profile are for friends and which parts are for work contacts.

✔ You can add people to your circles without needing them to add you as a friend in return. In this way, you can follow professional contacts without requesting their permission.

✔ You can use the Translate tool to follow what is happening on profiles in other languages.

What to watch out for when using Google+:

✔ Employers and recruiters searching for candidates don't use Google+ as a standard tool the way they use LinkedIn.

✔ Google+ has a lot more to it than pretty much any other social media platform, so it takes more time and effort to understand all the features and how to use them before getting started.

Playing it safe online

Many people use social media without giving a thought to their security. Protecting your identity, your privacy and the privacy of the people in your network requires your attention, so listen up. Social media also exposes you to receiving spam (unwanted advertising) and even computer viruses. We don't want to scare you — just compel you to spend a few extra moments to stay safe online by following these simple steps:

✔ Check the security and privacy settings on the social media pages you use. For example, much of your Facebook profile is public by default. If you don't want a recruiter or potential employer browsing your personal updates and viewing your photos and videos, apply the available security settings. To do this, go to Account→Privacy Settings→Friends Only. When an employer searches for you via Google or Bing they won't be able to view your profile or see your personal status updates or photos.

✔ Most people want recruiters and employers to be able to view their details on LinkedIn. However, check out the Privacy Settings page anyway by moving your cursor over the small profile picture of you in the top right corner of the homepage and then select Privacy & Settings. This way,

you can make sure your profile is set up so that it's available to all the right people, just the way you want it. Considering who has full access to your networks is important. You may not want to share all your contacts with some connections.

✔ Consider carefully any invitation to connect that comes from someone you don't know, particularly on your Facebook page.

✔ Think before you click on a link sent to you by a trusted contact if it looks odd. It could be a trap sent by a stranger using their name, and by clicking on the link you could unleash a virus. For example, on Twitter you may receive a tempting tweet with a link such as, 'I've seen something awful about you on this website' or 'You'd better view this photograph of you'. Contact the person by email or phone and ask whether they sent you anything, but don't click on the link. A trusted contact would likely never send a blunt message like that.

✔ Don't post your contact details publicly. Also, ensure you're not disclosing anything private about your employer when posting information about your job, especially when sharing your work duties and responsibilities.

Creating the Perfect Social Media Profile

Your social media profile should be bursting with useful and fascinating information about you. It should also feature lots of relevant keywords. Your profile should sing your praises: Showcasing your career history and achievements is what a professional social media profile is all about. You're including the same information you would display in your resume, but you can take the self-promotion up a notch. Just ensure that all the information is genuine as well as positive. Be sure to plug any work history gaps. A profile that is only half done will leave people wondering what you're trying to hide. Make sure you cover off all the key areas such as work history, qualifications and membership of associations, and include some work samples if you can. Sites such as LinkedIn let you know when your profile is 100 per cent complete. Having a complete profile will maximise your opportunity of being found.

Also, keep adding to your profile by ensuring your contact details are current, you're expanding your network of connections and you're sharing useful work-related information, whether that be a link to an interesting article or video or your review of using a new tool or device.

When you get started with a new social media platform, ensure you have the time to maintain your new profile. Each social media profile requires regular activity so it doesn't become dated or look neglected. If your job title is out of date, or you haven't posted a comment or update in months, it works against your personal brand, implying a lack of interest rather than presenting you as the dynamic professional you really are.

In this section, we explore how to create an effective social media profile to enhance your career prospects, using a LinkedIn profile as an example.

Getting started

Start your social media profile with a succinct personal profile summary that outlines who you are. To give you a couple of examples of how to create a profile summary on LinkedIn, we provide our own profiles as they were at the time of publication. Note our advice elsewhere in this chapter: Social media profiles need to be constantly reviewed and updated. So, if you see us online somewhere and our profiles have changed, you'll know we have taken our own advice!

Kate's profile encapsulates her *portfolio career*. A portfolio career means you have more than one career on the go at the same time. In Kate's case, that means being a journalist, a communications consultant and a career coach.

Kate Southam's profile summary:

> Journalist, Communications Consultant and Careers & Employment Coach. Key skills: research, interviewing and writing (internal and external communications, editorial and advertorial articles, blogs, newsletters and website copy); producing corporate videos; speaker and live presenter; and coaching both individual clients and groups (on public speaking, business writing skills, career planning, workplace issues, attracting and managing staff, employment branding).

Amanda's profile includes her accomplishments upfront, links to examples of her work and includes lots of wonderful keywords to showcase her specialties.

Amanda McCarthy's profile summary:

> HR practitioner with a background in recruitment, training and project coordination. For the past couple of years I have undertaken HR and career-related assignments in both the private and public sectors. I enjoy project work and assisting individuals transform their lives and reach their career goals.

Some of my career highlights have included:

- Author of *Australian Resumes For Dummies* (1st edition).

- Operated my own small business.

- Published articles on the MyCareer website and was featured in *National Accountant* magazine, *Gympie Times* and *Sunshine Coast Daily* newspapers.

- Designed and delivered *Getting that Job* training to Department of Communities employees throughout Queensland. (Click on the links to see work examples.)

Next, add your current job, including your job title and the name of your employer, or simply list your job role. Then add your career history in reverse chronological order, just as you do when creating your resume. Too easy! Include your education, skills, certifications, awards and memberships, and list your blog if you have one. As you start joining relevant LinkedIn groups, these appear in your profile too, rounding you out as an active professional in your industry.

Remember to feature keywords reflecting the terms commonly used in your profession to help you get noticed by employers. Refer to Chapter 4 for some examples of suitable keywords for different types of role.

Never fake a degree, falsify dates of employment or exaggerate past job titles. Your social media profile lives in the public domain so any fib is easily spotted. Your connections (particularly former bosses and colleagues) know exactly what you did in prior roles. Not only that, recruitment firms headhunting you will verify information through referee and professional qualification checks down the track. Don't be sneaky — honesty is always the best policy.

Use keywords sensibly. Some people are overly repetitive with their use of a particular keyword in the hope they'll turn up more often in search results. This will backfire on you. Experienced recruiters will know what you are up to while the less social media savvy may view your repetition as an example of poor writing or proofreading skills.

Keeping your audience in mind

When creating your profile, keep in mind how it will serve you. On the one hand, employers searching for professionals in your sector should be able to find and assess your skills and qualifications easily. Imagining yourself as an employer assessing your profile is a good way to test whether the information is useful and relevant. On the other hand, you will be directing people to your profile in a number of ways. When meeting people at work functions, you could invite people to stay in touch by connecting with you on LinkedIn. You can also invite current and former work colleagues, business contacts and even people you studied with to connect with you. You may also wish to proactively point to your profile on your resume.

Just include your LinkedIn profile name on your resume at the end of your contact details, for example:

Bill Wong

0438 560 123

`bill.wong@emaildomain.com.au`

`http://www.linkedin.com/in/billwong`

Keeping your audience in mind will help guide you as you populate your profile with details from your work history, education and training, memberships of associations and organisations and link to examples of your work. Would you hire you?

Also, pick a spelling and stick to it throughout your profile. Don't use American spelling in some areas and British spelling in another. If your target audience will be mainly in Australia and New Zealand, stick with British spelling — for example, 'organisation' rather than 'organization'.

When adding a position you've held to your career history, why not also add something you achieved in that role? Not everyone does this so it will help you stand out.

Picture perfect: Choosing the right photograph

Unlike resumes in Australia and New Zealand, where including a photograph would be seen as unusual, connecting your name with your face is the norm on social media. According to research by LinkedIn, having a profile picture increases your odds of getting viewed.

However, there is definitely a right way and a wrong way to go about creating the right image. Here are some quick tips for creating that perfect image:

- Choosing a 'head and shoulders' photo of yourself works far better than a full body shot or any image shot from a distance.

- Standing alone is the professional approach. Don't use a group shot.

- 'Selfies' or photos you take by pointing your mobile phone back at yourself can look awkward.

✔ Asking a friend to take a fresh, professional-looking shot of you only takes a few minutes.

✔ Recycling is great for the environment, but it doesn't work as well for photos. Men are advised not to crop themselves out of their wedding photo — we can tell — and women, that sarong and sunburn screams holiday snap!

While these days tattoos and piercings are favoured by a wide range of people from all walks of life, if you're applying for jobs in more conservative professions such as banking, accounting or law consider covering up when creating your profile photo. You don't necessarily need to cover your body art, however, if you're applying for a job in a creative team, the trade sector or — obviously — if you're chasing a job as a tattoo artist.

Avoid using photos that are old. You want the employer or recruiter to be able to recognise you when you turn up for the job interview. Also, update your profile photo if you change your look dramatically, such as going from blonde to brunette.

Linking to examples of your work

Linking to examples of your work is a great way to stand out from the crowd when job hunting, and is something you generally can't do from a resume. Work samples could include linking to a website or social media page where your work is displayed, linking to a PDF document or even to a video of you presenting at a seminar or conference. However, keep these few things in mind:

✔ Make sure none of the work you're linking to is confidential or commercially sensitive.

✔ If the work sample was a shared project, ask for the permission of the relevant parties before posting it on your professional social media profile.

✔ Be sure to safeguard the privacy of anyone whose name or identity may be revealed when including a link to your work sample.

You should also take the time to personalise your URL rather than use a generic one. This means your name will appear as part of the URL, so for Bill Wong (from our previous example) his URL is:

```
http://www.linkedin.com/in/billwong
```

Without personalising your URL it won't mention your name. By personalising your LinkedIn ID you make yourself easier to find and you can use your URL in your resume.

To personalise your LinkedIn URL:

1. **Sign in to LinkedIn.**

   Your LinkedIn home page appears.

2. **Hover over the profile button with your mouse and select Edit Profile from the drop-down menu.**

   On the editable profile page that appears, you'll see your LinkedIn ID underneath your profile picture.

3. **Click the Edit option.**

   A new screen appears where you can edit your public profile.

4. **On the right side, under the Customize Your Public Profile section, in the smaller section titled Your Public Profile URL, select Customize Your Public Profile URL.**

   The Customize Your Public Profile URL pop-up box appears.

5. **Personalise your URL by typing your preferred URL in the text box, and clicking on Set Custom URL.**

Some people also use sites such as LinkedIn to promote the products and services their current company offers. They may introduce themselves in a career profile then include a blurb on the organisation, its industry and what it specialises in. Some even link to the company's website for more information.

Asking others to sing your praises

LinkedIn allows people to recommend you and write short testimonials about their experiences of working with you. People can also Endorse a particular skill you have by just clicking on a button. Recommendations and endorsements are a great way to bring your career history to life.

Ask someone who knows your work well to provide you with a recommendation. Be aware, however, that doing so can feel awkward. Another way to go about this is to wait until people spontaneously provide you with positive feedback in the course of your work, and then ask if they would mind turning that email or phone call into a LinkedIn recommendation.

Keeping Your Profile Fresh: Using Social Media to Your Advantage

Social media is a highly useful and even vital tool in your job search and for building your career. However, like everything else in life it does take work. If you allow a social media profile to languish, it will look uncared for and out-of-date instead of energised and impressive. What doesn't serve you could harm you so if you create a profile, make sure you look after it.

Frequent social media interaction is key to your social media success. Keep your profile fresh and current by staying active online and regularly doing the following:

- ✔ Adding to your network by sending invitations to connect to people you know.

- ✔ Being selective about who you connect with and avoid accepting unsolicited invitations from people you don't know. It may be a scam.

- ✔ Keeping your profile fresh by updating new qualifications, industry memberships and promotions.

- ✔ Providing endorsements to others using the skills that most relate to their job preferences, which usually leads to return endorsements for you.

- ✔ Asking for LinkedIn recommendations when people send you positive emails about your work.

- ✔ Posting links to interesting articles or information that relates to your field.

- ✔ Contributing to the social media environment by participating in group discussions and blogs.

- ✔ Running regular analytics to see how many people or groups have been viewing your profile.

Set reminders in your online calendar to review and refresh your online social media profiles regularly and be sure to take an interest in new developments on each site. Additional features are added or improved regularly and are usually explained in easy-to-follow updates.

Your professional social media profile should be about work. Leave strong opinions to your personal Facebook page but even then keep your personal brand in mind. On your professional social media profile, making your posts, comments and other information useful to those in your network is the best way to build your profile.

Chapter 9

Dealing with Online Applications and Supporting Documents

· ·

In This Chapter

▶ Creating a dynamic portfolio

▶ Getting online application forms right

▶ Appending your results, qualifications and certificates

· ·

*G*etting a job these days requires extra effort. Sometimes you think you're ready just because you've crafted a standout resume. But wait, there's more! If you're going for a creative role, you need a stunning portfolio. And if you're applying for jobs in, say, the public service where online applications are not accepted, you need to complete an application cover sheet, address specific criteria ('selection criteria') outlined in the job ad, provide referees, and present a resume and well-constructed cover letter. Often, just filling in the forms, and photocopying and attaching the loads of extra documents that are required, seems like a full-time job. Phew!

In this chapter, we talk about all those bits and pieces that often accompany your resume when you're looking for jobs — portfolios, paper and online applications, and other supporting documentation that proves who you are and backs up your skills.

Promoting Your Portfolio

If you're seeking work as a copywriter, art director, graphic or web designer, architect, interior designer, teacher, photographer, illustrator or another creative role, you need to create a well-designed, eye-catching portfolio — like the one shown in Figure 9-1 — to show samples of your best work.

Figure 9-1: A portfolio, presented in PDF format.

We cover two types of portfolios in this section: Hard copy paper-based portfolios and digital portfolios.

Your portfolio — called folio for short — paints a picture of who you are and demonstrates to a recruiter the skills, knowledge, experience and creativity you have. It contains real-life samples of your work. Some examples of material you can present include:

Advertising campaigns	Packaging
Awards	Paintings
Brochures, posters, flyers, pamphlets, postcards, book, magazine and CD covers	Photographs
	Reports
Business stationery	Samples of student's work
Charts	Signage
Concept books/portfolios of ideas	Teaching materials
Drawings, illustrations, sketches, logos	Typography
Multimedia designs	Website designs
Newspaper or magazine articles	Writing samples

Here are some ideas to consider when you're deciding what to include in your portfolio:

✔ **Showcase your strongest work.** Be selective. Pick out a selection of pieces that best illustrate what you do well. Stun the recruiter with your creativity and extraordinary talent.

✔ **Express yourself.** Your portfolio needs to express your uniqueness — make sure it's original and represents who you are.

✔ **Cover the range.** Include pieces that show the gamut of your work experience (for example, direct mail, press ads, TV ads). Remember, variety is the spice of life.

- ✔ **Consider your audience.** Adapt your portfolio as needed, tailoring it to the job and company you're seeking to work for.

- ✔ **Show how concepts evolved.** Don't just focus on the end product. Include in your portfolio developmental sketches and process work.

- ✔ **Make your portfolio a living document.** Don't submit work that's old and tired. Keep your portfolio up to date and looking fresh. Display recent work that showcases your understanding of the latest software packages popular in your sector.

Hard copy portfolios

When you're applying for jobs, it's a good idea to have a hard copy of your portfolio ready to show recruiters. Presenting a collection of your work in a bound folder is a fantastic way to demonstrate who you are and highlight what you've achieved. Hard copy portfolios are particularly easy to use in job interviews.

Here are some tips for organising and presenting a hard copy portfolio:

- ✔ **Label each item.** Give each folio item a heading and brief description. For example, label your anti-smoking graphic design piece 'Brochure targeting young adults to quit smoking'. (You may like to include technical information as well, such as paper stock or the print run.)

- ✔ **Keep it flat.** Don't roll or fold your portfolio.

- ✔ **Make your name stand out.** Highlight your name or personal branding (logo) on each page of the folio so that recruiters don't confuse your work with someone else's.

- ✔ **Start with your strongest piece.** This engages the reader straightaway.

- ✔ **Don't think too big.** Make sure your portfolio is easy to carry and doesn't take up too much desk space. (A3 is the preferred size for large hard copy portfolios.)

- ✔ **Get the look right.** Think about the design of your portfolio pages and the placement of your pieces. Sequence your work so it flows. Remember, the appearance of your portfolio is very important; it showcases your design capabilities.

✔ **Keep things simple.** Don't go too over the top. Make sure your portfolio is well organised, easy to read and quick to flick through. The focus should be on the design work itself.

✔ **Create the right image.** If you're photographing your work samples, make sure you know how to use a camera properly, or otherwise pay a pro to take the shots for you. Poor lighting, blurred pictures and busy backgrounds will not do your artwork justice.

Always check with university or college lecturers, recruitment agencies or employers to find out the portfolio requirements for your industry.

Digital portfolios

Digital portfolios are a great way to show off your creative work, particularly if you have technical, graphic or web design skills. Not only can you scan in samples of your work or create a slide show of photographs of your work, but you can also take the 'wow' factor up a notch by adding sound, music, video and graphics.

Be careful about emailing your portfolio, particularly if it's packed full of graphics — the file may end up being very large and take a long time to download. You can always use a file-sharing service like You Send It or Dropbox. Be sure to ask the recruitment firm or employer the service it prefers to use.

Digital portfolios need to be submitted in a file format that the recruiter can open. The best option is to provide the recruiter with a PDF version of your portfolio (refer to Figure 9-1), delivered on USB if it's more than 2 megabytes in size. Again, ask if in any doubt about the best approach.

If you have your own website, blog or Instagram account showcasing your brilliance, simply provide the web address to the recruitment consultant or employer. Too easy! We explore using social media to complement your resume in Chapter 8.

Figure 9-2 shows an example of a web portfolio.

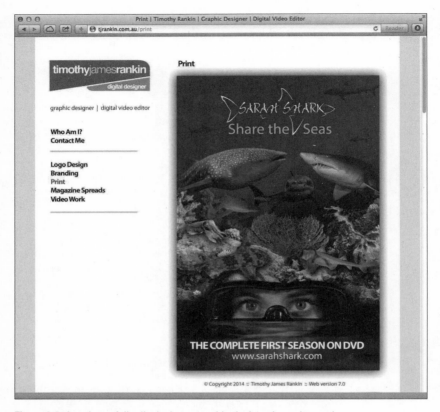

Figure 9-2: A web portfolio displaying a graphic designer's work samples.

The advantages of creating a digital portfolio are

- ✔ **Accessibility:** Employers can view web portfolios anytime.

- ✔ **Simple to store:** Digital portfolios take up less storage space than hard copy portfolios.

- ✔ **Ease of distribution:** Web-based portfolios are easy to pass on to other managers within the office.

- ✔ **Portability:** No need to lug around a bound folder, laptop or even rely on a hand-held device.

Don't rely solely on using a digital portfolio to impress employers. Although a digital portfolio may be a good way to gain an employer's attention, some recruiters like to see a hard copy of your portfolio in the interview. (Refer to the preceding section for more details.)

Filling in Application Forms

An application form is often required by employers when you send your resume, so be prepared to fill in forms when searching for jobs. You come across two main types of employment application forms on the job-hunting circuit: The paper-based variety and online forms. Both types allow recruiters to find out a little more about you and your experience.

Preparing hard copy applications

Some employers and recruiters still use hard copy application forms to shortlist and compare candidates. These forms are easy to analyse and enable the recruiter to find out valuable information about applicants — personal and educational details, work experience, skills, language proficiency and so on.

You can usually get your hands on a company's job application form by visiting the company directly or downloading the forms from its website. Some employers are happy for you to fill out hard copy forms, scan them in to your computer and email them back to be printed out at the other end. Have a chat with someone in the HR department or speak to a manager or supervisor to find out what their preference is. You may be able to take the application away with you, to complete in your own time. Some recruitment agencies also ask job seekers to fill in a paper-based application form as part of the registration process.

Employers recruiting large numbers of staff use recruitment days, where candidates turn up in person to apply for a job. It's pretty odds-on that in such cases you'll be asked to fill in an application form, but always bring your resume just in case.

Filling in the blanks

No matter what type of application form you're filling in, take note of these guidelines:

- ✔ **Use formal language.** Never abbreviate words, use acronyms, slang or casual lingo.

- ✔ **Don't rush.** Spend time completing the application form properly. Rushing your application may result in errors and you crashing out of contention for the job.

✔ **Proofread.** Always proofread what you've written before submitting. Nothing is worse than an application form riddled with typos and spelling mistakes, especially if the position requires attention to detail.

Here are some do's to consider when putting pen to paper:

✔ Take these things along with you to the company if you're completing an application form in person: Your reading glasses (if you need them), a copy of your resume and the details of your referees.

✔ Remember to dress in a neat and professional manner, even when applying for an outdoor-based or physically demanding role — first impressions do count.

✔ Read the form first and follow the instructions before you start writing, particularly if you're filling in the form at home. Photocopy a couple of applications to use as drafts and have a few trial runs. Try not to cram too much information into a small amount of space. Adapt your writing style or attach a separate sheet of paper.

✔ Be specific and mention the sort of work you're interested in, particularly if the company has different departments. Employers aren't mind-readers.

✔ Print, rather than use cursive writing. Printing is more legible.

✔ Fill in all sections as required. You can bet your bottom dollar recruiters will think the worst and wonder what you're hiding if you skip sections. Answer every question and use N/A (not applicable) if the answer doesn't apply to you.

✔ Stick to blue or black ink. These colours photocopy best.

✔ Make a photocopy for your own records (if you can). You may need it in the interview. Make sure you've signed and dated the form and go through each question one by one to check that you've completed it satisfactorily.

And just as important, make sure you don't:

✔ Lie or put in false dates — you'll be sorry when you're found out.

✔ Go nuts with the correction tape — too much can look really messy.

✔ Take the lazy option and use the term 'see resume' to fill in the blanks. Recruiters may find this frustrating — going back and forth between your resume and job application is a pain.

✔ Sign your life away without reading the declaration on the form carefully. If you are unsure about something, ask.

✔ Submit a tatty application form that is creased, smudged or tattooed with coffee stains. Save these copies for the bin. Neat, professional applications work wonders.

Logging on to online forms

Many organisations today, particularly larger ones, are moving away from the traditional paper applications and using online application forms to gather background information on applicants.

Accessing a specific company's online job application form usually requires visiting the company's website and first finding positions available by clicking on the Careers, Employment or Join Us link. This takes you to the company's main careers page.

Figure 9-3: Read the position description or job ad, then press 'Apply' to start the application process.

Here you can view current vacancies or use the site's search facility to browse for jobs. Many companies are also listing available jobs on their Facebook and LinkedIn profile pages, so be sure to check if they have profiles. When you find a job that interests you, click on the job title to view the ad or position description (as shown in Figure 9-3). Then click the Apply button to begin the application process.

The questions listed in online application forms are much the same as those provided on hard copy application forms. The difference is, when you're finished filling out the online form, you submit it electronically to the company.

Sometimes a Careers, Employment or Join Us link may not be immediately visible on the company's website. If this is the case, look for the site's About Us page or try looking under corporate information.

The important thing to note about online application forms is that they come in different shapes and sizes — each company has its own format and procedures for dealing with the recruitment process. Some online forms are simple; others

No-frills downloadable forms

Some websites offer simple, straightforward non-interactive forms (usually in PDF format) that you download from the company's site to complete. After you download the form you print it out, fill in your details by hand, then submit the form to the employer by email (by scanning the form), fax, post or in person.

Another variety is the basic fillable form you complete on screen. You type the information into the designated fields and, depending on the security settings indicated by the creator of the form, you can either print out the completed form, save a copy to your hard drive or send it back to the employer. To move from field to field, press the Tab key.

One reason an employer may use a fillable form is that, compared to a handwritten form, it's easier for the recruiter to read. Fillable forms are commonly created in Microsoft Word, Excel or PDF format.

To save a blank version of an Adobe form or to print copies of a completed form, you first need to download and install Adobe's free Acrobat reader software on your computer. For more information about Adobe Software, visit www.adobe.com.au.

include extra features so that you can save and edit your application before submitting it.

Some online application forms require you to register first, setting up an account in the process. Registering also gives you access to other benefits and services. For example, some company websites allow you to:

- Set up automatic email alerts, so that you'll be notified when any new jobs matching your search preferences become available
- Store your resume on the organisation's database
- Change your password
- Create a profile of yourself, so that your skills and experience can be matched to future job opportunities
- Track all your online job applications

The beauty of these online forms is that you don't need to complete the job application in one session. You can fill out all or just a part of the application, save a draft copy and come back to the form at a later date. We show you an example of this type of application form in Figure 9-4.

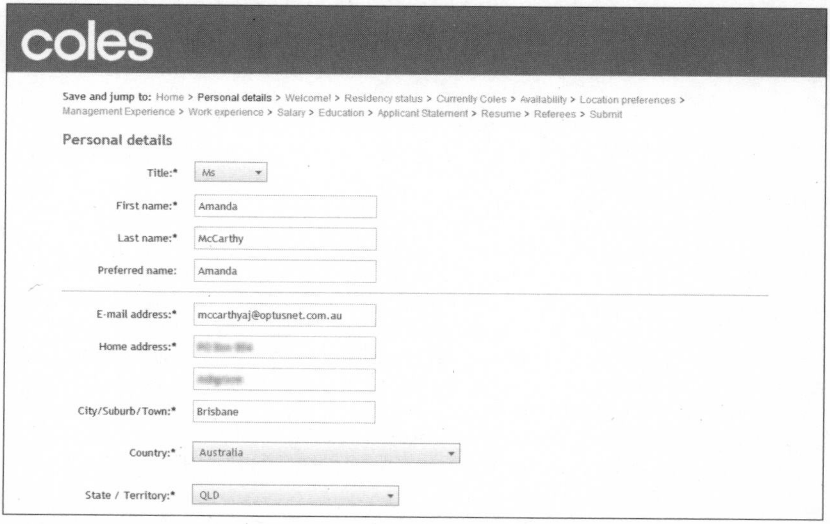
coles

Save and jump to: Home > Personal details > Welcome! > Residency status > Currently Coles > Availability > Location preferences > Management Experience > Work experience > Salary > Education > Applicant Statement > Resume > Referees > Submit

Personal details

Title:* Ms

First name:* Amanda

Last name:* McCarthy

Preferred name: Amanda

E-mail address:* mccarthyaj@optusnet.com.au

Home address:*

City/Suburb/Town:* Brisbane

Country:* Australia

State / Territory:* QLD

Figure 9-4: An online form that allows you to create your application in stages.

Online application forms like the example shown in Figure 9-4 have different sections you must complete before you submit your application. If you fail to include all the necessary information on the page, the system alerts you by highlighting the incomplete or missing fields.

To return to your online application at a later time, you simply log in on the company's website using the username (or email address) and password you created when you registered. You can then view or withdraw your incomplete application, change your password, check and monitor the progress of submitted applications, and update your profile and resume. (For tips on editing and completing the online application process, see the following section.)

Completing an online application form

Here are some things to consider before submitting a job application online. Make sure you

- ✔ Read the questions properly and think through your answers before filling in the fields. For example, if you're asked 'Why do you want to work for our organisation?' don't say 'Because I need a job' (even if this is the case). Some questions may be designed to screen you out of the process automatically.

- ✔ Research the role prior to filling out the application form — gather info about the employer and the job. Have this information and any other supporting documentation on hand when you're applying for jobs.

- ✔ List your correct email address and contact details. To complete an online application you do need a valid email address. If you don't have one, set up a free web-based email account at Yahoo! or Google. (Remember to check your account regularly to keep it active.) Also, if you're using a web-based email address, make sure job-related emails can reach you and are not filtered out as spam. Email addresses are often used for logging-on purposes. Most companies will acknowledge receipt of your application through an automatic email confirmation.

✔ Copy and paste your resume in the file format the employer requests (for more details, see the following section). Note that if you paste a word-processed resume into an online form, some of the formatting may be lost. To avoid formatting problems occurring, convert your document to plain text format.

✔ Save your work regularly (if you can). Some systems will time-out after a period of inactivity. Don't risk losing your information. If you're in the middle of an application and want to complete it later, save your work first, then exit the form.

✔ Upload your resume or cover letter in the file format requested (for example, .doc, .docx, .pdf, .rtf, .txt or html). Ensure your documents are current.

✔ Make a note of your applicant number (if one is given).

And, of course, some don'ts. When submitting an online application, try not to

✔ Select passwords you'll never remember. Keep track of all your user name and passwords, particularly if you're applying for a few jobs. Alternatively, use the same login name for each site you register with — this makes remembering easy!

✔ Submit your application without printing off the form. If possible, keep a copy of your completed application for future records.

Sizing up selection criteria

Private, public sector and not-for-profit organisations often require you to address selection criteria as part of the written application process. Selection criteria are standards used to select the best person for the job. The trick to mastering selection criteria is not to give up. You need to show how well you meet each one, proving you have the skills, knowledge, qualifications and experience they're looking for. In Chapter 13, we give you detailed information on how to address selection criteria or key capabilities in the public sector.

Uploading your resume with an online form

Some organisations use an online application form in lieu of a resume: You enter your personal details, experience, education, referees and so on into the set fields of the form, but the application form doesn't accept resume or cover letter attachments. Other companies, however, may require you to complete an online application, then ask you to attach your resume to the form. If you're asked to attach your resume, you simply click on the Browse button located on the online form, select the appropriate drive on your computer and choose your resume file name, then click on the Attach or Upload button on-screen to upload your document.

Alternatively, the online application form may offer a few different ways to upload your resume. For example, you may be able to upload an existing resume, or copy and paste your resume into the online form, or create one from scratch by filling in the blank fields of the online form.

Appending Your Supporting Documents

You may be required to submit further material to support your job application and resume when applying for a position — especially if you're a schoolie, just starting out in the workforce, or a uni student applying for graduate programs. You may have to provide a copy of your tertiary entrance results, qualifications, academic record or a transcript of your results. Similarly, if you're looking for work in the trades, recruiters will need to sight and photocopy your trade certificate. Other documents you may need to provide include current registrations and licences and training certificates — for example, safety training certificates.

If you're required to send in a hard copy application, never ever post in original copies of your certificates or qualifications for jobs. Send only photocopies. Don't run the risk of your most treasured possessions getting damaged, ripped or lost in the post.

Keep several photocopies of each of your important documents, witnessed or certified by a justice of the peace (JP) or solicitor, if required. You can track down a justice of the peace in banks, law firms, police stations, courthouses, government departments, shopping centres, real estate agencies and local, state and federal members' offices. Ask around your personal network or search online in your local area under 'justice of the peace'.

Registrations

Signing up for jobs in fields such as teaching often requires you to include with your application evidence of your current registration. This verifies that you're an authentic, true-blue professional.

Tickets and licences

When you register with agencies for industrial work, particularly jobs involving big toys such as cranes, dozers, front-end loaders, forklifts or other heavy plant machinery, you may be asked to show proof of your tickets or licences in the interview. Recruitment consultants may need to view and attach these documents to your personnel records before they let you loose on job sites.

Driving history report

If you are on the lookout for truck, bus or ambulance driving work, you may come across employers and recruitment agencies that require you to attach an extract of your driving record to your job application. Requirements vary depending on the country and area where you are looking for work, but usually this involves visiting your nearest traffic authority and requesting a printout of your traffic and driver's licence history.

Construction industry induction training

In most places, workplace health and safety laws require compulsory health and safety induction training for construction workers. So, if you're looking for ongoing work on construction sites, this means you need to show proof of your safety training to a prospective employer or recruitment consultant. Cards are commonly issued as evidence of induction training.

For more information on construction industry induction training, contact WorkCover or the workplace health and safety (WHS) authority in your state or territory. See Table 9-1 for contact details within Australia and New Zealand.

Table 9-1   WHS Regulatory Authorities — Australia and New Zealand

State/ Country	State Authority	Contact Details
ACT	WorkSafe ACT	(02) 6207 3000 www.workcover.act.gov.au
NSW	WorkCover NSW	131050 www.workcover.nsw.gov.au
NT	NT WorkSafe	1800 019 115 www.worksafe.nt.gov.au
QLD	Workplace Health & Safety QLD	1300 369 915 (Info line) www.deir.qld.gov.au/workplace
SA	SafeWork SA	1300 365 255 www.safeworksa.gov.au
TAS	Workplace Standards Tasmania	1300 135 513 workplacestandards.tas.gov.au/
VIC	WorkSafe Victoria	1800 136 089 or (03) 9641 1444 www.worksafe.vic.gov.au
WA	WorkSafe Western Australia	1300 307 877 www.worksafe.wa.gov.au
New Zealand	WorkSafe New Zealand	0800 030 040 (free call) or (04) 897 7699 (international callers) www.worksafe.govt.nz

Driver's licence and birth certificates

Many occupations, such as the police force, fire brigade or the teaching profession, require you to attach a copy of your driver's licence or birth certificate to your employment application form. This is for proof of identity.

A copy of a driver's licence is mandatory in a job that requires the employee to drive on the road — whether you're an ambulance officer responding to emergencies, a bus driver transporting passengers, a truck driver delivering freight or a firefighter attending to fires.

First aid certificates

If your dream job is helping to look after kids in a childcare centre, or run a gym, or you've always wanted to be a tour guide operator and take people bushwalking, you may need to show evidence of a current first aid certificate.

Passport, visas and citizenship

For some jobs, you may be asked to submit proof of your citizenship, permanent residency or your right to work in Australia or New Zealand. This is often a key requirement for ambulance paramedics, pilots or police positions. Also, if you're visiting Australia or New Zealand from another country and are registering with recruitment agencies for temporary work, remember to bring along to the interview your resume, work visa, passport, bank account details and tax file number. Recruitment consultants will need to take a copy of your passport and work visa and place it in your personnel record, along with your resume and other employment documentation.

Part IV

Sampling from the Suite of Resumes

Brand Manager

Contact

Lachlan James Dunn
27/318 Palace Road
LANE COVE NSW 2066

H: 02 2222 2222
M: 2222 2222

Status: Australian Citizen

Education

2005 — University of New South Wales
Bachelor of Commerce (Marketing)

Achievements Prize for 1st place in
Strategic Marketing

Employment Summary

Dates	Employer	Position Held
Jan 2006 to Current	House Clean Pty Ltd	
Jul 2009 to Current	House Clean Pty Ltd	Brand Manager, Bathroom Cleaners
Jan 2006 to Jul 2009	House Clean Pty Ltd	Assistant Brand Manager, Kitchen Cleaners

Interests

Equity markets, dining out, rugby union, cricket, basketball, current affairs and theatre.

Employment History

Jan 2006 to Current — **House Clean Pty Ltd**

House Clean Pty Ltd is the largest manufacturer and marketer of household cleaning products in Australia. It boasts a turnover in excess of $300 million and a market share of 22% of the Australian household cleaning market. The company markets products such as No Elbow Grease, Sparkling and Proud Family.

Jul 2009 to Current — **Brand Manager, Bathroom Cleaners**

Reporting to a Marketing Manager, I hold the position of Brand Manager, Bathroom Cleaners. The portfolio is the second largest (by volume) in the company and commands a market share of 26.5% (MAT Jan 09). It has an advertising and promotion budget of $7.3 million.

In this role, my key responsibilities are:

- Develop an insightful understanding via analysis and review of all available data sources (scan data, ad hoc market research, competitor and overseas market review) of the consumer and the market for bathroom cleaners.
- Develop a 1- and 3-year brand plan and secure executive approval.
- Brief, manage and deliver all agreed brand activities including TV and other media advertising development, media planning, sales promotion, pricing and account promotional plan, account specific pack development and new product development.
- Ensure that agreed volume, $ per kg, cost of goods sold and profit targets and ratios are achieved.

In this role, my key achievements have been:

- Grew brand volume by 6.8% versus total segment growth rate of 3.4% and thus grew volume market share by 23.5% to 26.5%.
- Identified new consumer insight that led to development of the 'Elbow Strain' TV campaign, a key driver of the increase in heavy user consumption which underpinned volume growth.
- Developed two new, on-pack sales promotions that were amongst the most successful 5 promotions run on the brand in the last decade.

Jan 2006 to Jul 2009 — **Assistant Brand Manager, Kitchen Cleaners**

Reporting to the Marketing Manager, Kitchen Cleaners, I held the position of Assistant Brand Manager, Kitchen Cleaners. The kitchen cleaning portfolio is the fastest growing and most profitable part of the company.

In this role, my key responsibilities were:

- Developed a thorough understanding of all key marketing disciplines by providing assistance to the Marketing Manager in all brand planning and activation activities.
- Managed all sales and budget analysis and monthly reporting.

In this role, my key achievement has been the identification of an account specific opportunity for a 1kg SKU, which I developed and launched. This SKU has exceeded its volume targets and has grown total company sales in the account at 50% above market rate.

Referees — Available on request

(1 of 2)   (2 of 2)

Source: Talent2 (with adaptations).

Discover more information about sample resumes at `www.dummies.com/extras/writingresumescoverlettersau`.

In this part...

- ✔ Review example resumes for a variety of different industries — and use these samples to help you create your own standout resume.

- ✔ Land your first job once you leave school.

- ✔ Focus on the detail to enhance your graduate resume.

- ✔ Manage the application process for a public sector role.

Chapter 10

A Sampling of Standout Resumes

. . . .

In This Chapter

▶ Understanding the resume details that recruiters look for

▶ Looking at sample resumes for different career fields

. . . .

*I*n this chapter, we share resume samples provided by top recruitment agencies or adapted from resumes we've created or revised in our years of helping job hunters. All names and personal details have been changed to protect the identity of the job hunter in question, and the email addresses and many of the company names are made up. Most of the schools, universities, colleges, qualifications, course names, training providers and professional associations are real, however.

These resumes all get the stamp of approval for a number of reasons:

✔ They are business-like and easy to read, with clear headings and lots of white space.

✔ Contact details are visible — employers and recruitment agencies must be able to get in touch with ease to arrange an interview.

✔ The candidate's work history is listed in reverse chronological order (starting with the most recent job first).

✔ Dates of employment are written in months and years, instead of just years — much easier for a hiring manager or recruitment consultant to follow.

✔ Responsibilities are written clearly and succinctly. Achievements attract an employer or recruitment consultant's attention. These both show that the candidate 'walks the talk' and has added value to past employers' organisations.

✔ Most include a career profile or employment summary near the top, tailored to the job being applied for, which allows the reader to quickly see that the candidate is shortlist material. (We discuss career profiles in more detail in Chapter 3.)

✔ Company descriptions help the candidate demonstrate the types of companies they have worked for, which is particularly useful for employers that are not well known.

Using a company description can be particularly useful for candidates coming from overseas. Pointing out that your employer was the largest hospital in the region or the fastest growing technology firm will help the person assessing your application put your experience in a local context.

✔ Stating you have the right to work in Australia or New Zealand can make it easy for the recruitment consultant or employer to progress your application. You will see in our first example that the candidate has stated he is an Australian citizen.

Brand Manager

Contact	Lachlan James Dunn 27/318 Palace Road LANE COVE NSW 2066 H: 02 2222 2222 M: 2222 2222 Status: Australian Citizen
Education	
2005	University of New South Wales Bachelor of Commerce (Marketing) Achievements Prize for 1st place in Strategic Marketing

Employment Summary

Dates	Employer	Position Held
Jan 2006 to Current	House Clean Pty Ltd	
Jul 2009 to Current	House Clean Pty Ltd	Brand Manager, Bathroom Cleaners
Jan 2006 to Jul 2009	House Clean Pty Ltd	Assistant Brand Manager, Kitchen Cleaners

Interests	Equity markets, dining out, rugby union, cricket, basket-ball, current affairs and theatre.

Employment History

Jan 2006 to Current	**House Clean Pty Ltd** **House Clean Pty Ltd** is the largest manufacturer and marketer of household cleaning products in Australia. It boasts a turnover in excess of $300 million and a market share of 22% of the Australian household cleaning market. The company markets products such as No Elbow Grease, Sparkling and Proud Family.
Jul 2009 to Current	**Brand Manager, Bathroom Cleaners** Reporting to a Marketing Manager, I hold the position of Brand Manager, Bathroom Cleaners. The portfolio is the second largest (by volume) in the company and commands a market share of 26.5% (MAT Jan 09). It has an advertising and promotion budget of $7.3 million.

In this role, my key responsibilities are:

- Develop an insightful understanding via analysis and review of all available data sources (scan data, ad hoc market research, competitor and overseas market review) of the consumer and the market for bathroom cleaners.
- Develop a 1- and 3-year brand plan and secure executive approval.
- Brief, manage and deliver all agreed brand activities including TV and other media advertising development, media planning, sales promotion, pricing and account promotional plan, account specific pack development and new product development.
- Ensure that agreed volume, $ per kg, cost of goods sold and profit targets and ratios are achieved.

In this role, my key achievements have been:

- Grew brand volume by 6.8% versus total segment growth rate of 3.4% and thus grew volume market share by 23.5% to 26.5%.
- Identified new consumer insight that led to development of the 'Elbow Strain' TV campaign, a key driver of the increase in heavy user consumption which underpinned volume growth.
- Developed two new, on-pack sales promotions that were amongst the most successful 5 promotions run on the brand in the last decade.

Jan 2006 to Jul 2009

Assistant Brand Manager, Kitchen Cleaners

Reporting to the Marketing Manager, Kitchen Cleaners, I held the position of Assistant Brand Manager, Kitchen Cleaners. The kitchen cleaning portfolio is the fastest growing and most profitable part of the company.

In this role, my key responsibilities were:

- Developed a thorough understanding of all key marketing disciplines by providing assistance to the Marketing Manager in all brand planning and activation activities.
- Managed all sales and budget analysis and monthly reporting.

In this role, my key achievement has been the identification of an account specific opportunity for a 1kg SKU, which I developed and launched. This SKU has exceeded its volume targets and has grown total company sales in the account at 50% above market rate.

Referees

Available on request

Source: Talent2 (with adaptations).

Acquisitions Manager (Property)

Adam Reynolds

35 Symons Rd,
St Lucia Qld 4067

M: 0402 xxx xxx   E: adamreynolds@email.com.au

Career Profile

Top-performing, proactive Acquisitions Manager with expertise in residential, commercial development and property valuation, I have experience in feasibilities, town planning, cash flow analysis, legal and taxation issues. With outstanding communication, negotiation and relationship-building skills, I have a proven record of identifying and bringing to life successful development opportunities. I also possess a thorough knowledge of the property market as well as a degree in property economics.

Professional Experience

ACQUISITIONS MANAGER,   June 2009 – Present
CARLINGTON DEVELOPMENT GROUP, Gold Coast
About Carlington Development Group: One of Australia's largest developers of commercial, retail, residential and industrial property, the company employs more than 300 people across Queensland, Victoria and New South Wales.

Reporting to: CEO

Key Responsibilities:

- Plan, develop and implement the acquisitions strategy for South-East Queensland.
- Research property trends, analyse market conditions and monitor competitor's activities, as well as prepare purchase business cases for submission to the Board of Directors.
- Establish business relationships with real estate agents and property owners to access development sites and coordinate inspections.
- Perform due diligence reviews on potential sites, negotiate contracts with solicitors and work with engineers, consultants and project managers.

Key Achievements:

- Negotiated the acquisition of 800 allotments worth more than $120M over just a nine-month period.
- Developed and leveraged key relationships with a group of owners to secure much sought after parcels of land zoned for commercial development for the first time.
- Created a quarterly networking breakfast for real estate agents and property owners featuring a different industry-leading speaker.

ACQUISITIONS MANAGER,   August 2005 – May 2009
HENDERSON PROPERTIES, Brisbane
About Henderson Properties: Prominent residential property development company selling land and house-only packages to prospective purchasers. The company employs over 400 staff with offices in New South Wales, Victoria, Queensland and South Australia.

(1 of 3)

Reported to: General Manager

Key Responsibilities:

- Investigated and assessed potential sites and then negotiated and acquired major land parcels for residential development and master-planned communities.
- Performed feasibility and cash flow analysis using Estate Master.
- Undertook town planning, engineering, geotechnical and environmental investigations on properties.
- Worked closely with solicitors and negotiated the terms and conditions of legal contracts with vendors.
- Prepared and submitted comprehensive land acquisition proposals to the Board of Directors for sign-off.
- Consulted and negotiated with councils concerning infrastructure issues, development applications, terms and conditions of development approval and other issues pertaining to specific land parcels.

Key Achievements:

- Secured $140M in residential property within eight months through property knowledge and strong business networks.
- Recipient of the Henderson Properties Star Quality Award (March 2006). This is a quarterly staff award for outstanding performance.
- Selected to attend a major conference on property development in Queensland in July 2006 and then make a presentation to senior management about conference highlights.

COMMERCIAL PROPERTY VALUER,   March 2002 – July 2005
BICKFORD PROPERTY GROUP, Brisbane

About Bickford: Property valuation firm with over 50 employees providing commercial, plant and equipment property valuation services to clients throughout Queensland.

Reported to: General Manager

Key Responsibilities:

- Investigated and assessed the value of commercial properties, taking into account size, age, area, location, market, terms of lease, rent reviews, cash flow and the condition of the property.
- Performed commercial property valuations for hotels, leagues clubs, retail and commercial office buildings.
- Provided valuation of major residential land subdivisions.
- Compiled valuation reports and undertook residual cash flow analysis.

ASSISTANT VALUER,
ASHTON VALUATIONS, Brisbane   June 2001 – March 2002

Reported to: Commercial Valuer

Key Responsibilities:

- Researched market trends and performed valuations of residential, industrial, commercial and retail properties up to $2M.
- Conducted progress inspections for buildings under construction for mortgage security purposes.

Education

QUEENSLAND UNIVERSITY OF TECHNOLOGY, Brisbane   2000
Bachelor of Applied Science (Property Economics)

Memberships

- Member, Valuers Registration Board of Queensland
- Member, Urban Development Institute of Australia

Professional Registrations

- Registered with Australian Valuation Office

Activities

Cycling, triathlons, swimming, investing, renovating houses

Referees

Will be provided upon request

(3 of 3)

Source: Reproduced with permission from John Jameson.

Company Solicitor

Nicola Hughes

5 Dillon Street,
Paddington NSW 2021
| **h:** 02 9331 XXXX | **m:** 0482 XXXX |
ellawhite@email.com

Qualifications

Degrees	**Year**
• Graduate Diploma in Legal Practice (with merit) (University of Sydney)	2001
• Bachelor of Laws, Bachelor of Science (University of Western Sydney)	2000

Admitted to legal practice

• New South Wales	2002
• Australian Capital Territory and the High Court of Australia	2001

Employment History

Head of Legal (Company Solicitor)   (March 2009 – Current)
Blue Digital Solutions

*Blue Digital Solutions is a highly successful privately owned firm delivering
web-based e-commerce solutions with a staff of 110. Heading a team of three,
my department oversees contractual agreements, meets regulatory obligations
and licensing arrangements for software.*

Responsibilities include:

➤ **(legal advice)** providing legal advice and documentation for all operational
areas of Blue Digital Solutions, including creating contracts with clients and
suppliers, due diligence on major acquisitions, overseeing the creation of
licensing arrangements for the company's software products, and all other
commercial contracts.

➤ **(compliance)** identifying and minimising legal risks to Digital Blue Solutions,
including developing appropriate compliance procedures, providing training
and finding pragmatic solutions to litigious and commercial problems.

➤ **(drafting and negotiation)** reviewing, drafting and negotiating a wide
range of commercial documents and contracts such as sale and purchase
agreements, supplier contracts, leases, deeds of settlement, confidentiality
agreements, board reports, etc.

➤ **(management)** day to day management of a team of two lawyers
and a paralegal (skill development, mentoring, team management) and
management of a significant legal budget.

➤ **(strategy)** providing strategic input as a member of the senior leadership
team (direct report to Digital Blue Solutions CEO).

(1 of 3)

Achievements:

➤ Successfully negotiated and managed a variety of acquisitions, including Digital Images Inc and Finance Gateways Ltd.

➤ Established a matter management system that reduced legal risk, improved control of matters, and enabled better analysis of external expenditure and reporting to the business.

➤ Developed a precedent supplier contract and terms and conditions for the majority of Digital Blue Solutions suppliers.

➤ Increased service level of legal team by creating a new work delivery system resulting in a 18% increase in productivity without increasing staff hours.

Senior Associate   (Feb 2006 – Feb 2009)
Elias Brown & Associates

Headquartered in Sydney, Elias Brown & Associates is a boutique law firm specialising in intellectual property and licensing for internet products and services across global territories. As Senior Associate, my key area of responsibility was drafting intellectual property agreements for our clients. I also provided advice to in-house and external clients on a range of compliance issues.

Relevant skills, experience and achievements:

➤ **(research and knowledge sharing)** I worked directly with the firm's partner regarded as the subject matter expert on intellectual property. I travelled to the US several times to attend international conferences on emerging trends in intellectual property in the software sector, and presented at in-house and client events on these developments.

➤ **(drafting and negotiating)** held significant responsibility for drafting, reviewing and negotiating intellectual property agreements for several fast growing software clients.

➤ **(technical experience)** achieved high level of corporate technical expertise in all aspects of intellectual property agreements and compliance issues, in particular:

  ▪ **corporate compliance** — regularly advised listed companies on Corporations Act and ASX Listing Rules requirements including continuous disclosure, director's duties, capital raisings and restructurings, and managed internal company secretariat.

  ▪ **IPO preparation** — worked closely with Fast Track Payment Gateways over 10 months in 2006 to get the company ready for public listing in 2007. I received a Staff Member of the Year award in January 2007 for this work.

Solicitor (Jul 2002 – Jan 2006)
Department of Trade & Investment

The Department's portfolio includes primary industries, resources, regional development and small business. I was a member of the in-house Legal Services team that provides a broad range of services, including corporate legal services, compliance, policy and licensing agreements.

Relevant skills and experience:

- **(policy)** researched and contributed to policy drafts on key areas of investment, including mining, agricultural, tourism and new technologies. I also prepared ministerials and other briefing papers for decision makers.
- **(drafting)** drafted a range of agreements and contracts representing the government with suppliers and clients including inter-country agreements.
- **(compliance)** all agreements, contracts and other official documentation had to be reviewed to ensure compliance with rules and conditions. This work required great attention to detail, sound legal knowledge, and 100% accuracy.

Other Achievements

■ Received a 'Women Making a Difference Award' in 2007 for my work providing legal services to youth living on the streets.

Memberships

■ Australian Corporate Lawyers Association

Personal Interests

■ Sailing, dog training and tennis

Referees

■ Available on request

(3 of 3)

Source: From the authors.

Apprentice Hair Stylist

MARCUS WILSON   5/128 High Street, Northcote VIC 3070
M: 0433 xxx xxx E: marcuswilson@email.com.au

CAREER OBJECTIVE
Building on my apprenticeship by securing a trainee stylist position in a busy, modern salon with a strong culture of client care and support for ongoing staff education. With experience in hairdressing, reception work and putting clients at ease, I hope to secure the opportunity to learn from experienced stylists. Career highlights to date include winning two awards for young stylists at the HBIA Hairdressing Championships and the IHS State Championships. I am always willing to assist the team and do whatever tasks need performing, from cleaning to client care.

EDUCATION & TRAINING
Certificate III in Hairdressing,
Biba Academy, 2012

Victorian Certificate of Education,
Whittlesea Secondary College, 2012

PROFESSIONAL SKILLS
Hairdressing:

- Cape up clients for cuts or chemical services.
- Mix and apply colours, shampoo, condition and rinse hair and colours.
- Cut, trim, style, wave, curl, braid, blow-dry, colour and lighten hair.
- Treat hair and scalp conditions, perform chemical straightening and relaxing.
- Wash, dry, fold and restock salon capes and towels, clean salon, work and basin areas, tidy trolleys, sterilise tools and maintain equipment.
- Consult with clients to discuss their specific hair care requirements and recommend products to meet their hair care needs.

Customer Service:

- Welcome clients on arrival to the salon and offer beverages and a selection of magazines.
- Perform reception duties, including answering telephone calls, returning messages, booking and confirming client appointments.
- Update and maintain client records.

(1 of 2)

MARCUS WILSON

M: 0433 xxx xxx E: marcuswilson@email.com.au

Professional skills (Continued)

- Unpack orders, mark off and display stock.
- Cross-sell and up-sell retail hair care products, beauty services and cosmetics to clients.
- Use point of sale equipment, operate an EFTPOS machine and process credit card and cash transactions.
- End of day reconciliations.

EMPLOYMENT HISTORY

Apprentice, André Hair Design, Sept 2013 – Present
Apprentice, Strandz Hair Studio, Feb 2013 – Sept 2013

VOLUNTARY EXPERIENCE

Entrant, HBIA Australian Hairdressing Championships, Melbourne, 2012, 2013
Qualified for HBIA Apprentice & Student Awards, Melbourne, 2013
Entrant, IHS State Championships, Melbourne, 2013
Entrant, Apprentice Cutting Competition, Hair Expo Australia, Sydney, 2013
Event Crew, Hair Expo Australia, Sydney, 2012

PRODUCT TRAINING

Stage 2 L'Oreal Colour Training course, April 2013
Goldwell Product Training, June 2013

AWARDS

- 1st place 'Junior Catwalk', IHS State Championships, 2013
- 2nd place 'Colour Me Fashion 2013 – Apprentices and Students', HBIA Australian Hairdressing Championships

REFEREES

Ms Wendy Marr, Manager, André Hair Design – W: 03 xxxx xxxx
M: 0438 xxx xxx

Mr Thomas Smith, Senior Stylist, Strandz Hair Studio – W: 03
xxxx xxxx M: 0414 xxx xxx

(2 of 2)

Source: From the authors.

IT Support/ Helpdesk

Joe Bowles
78 Kemp Avenue Mount Waverley VIC 3149
(03) 3333 3333 or 0311 111 111
jb@email.com.au

Summary

- Experienced IT professional with a background in helpdesk and desktop support.
- Familiar with call logging software, Windows 7, Windows NT, MS Office, Exchange, Novell, Outlook and Citrix.
- Strong analytical and troubleshooting skills.
- Able to work under pressure to resolve problems and requests within a specific time frame, or escalate complex issues to Level 2 specialists.
- Proven ability to prioritise issues in order of severity and importance, ensuring that business critical problems are resolved promptly.
- Able to work autonomously and in a team environment.
- Skilled in determining the cause rather than the symptom of a problem, enabling the timely resolution of issues.
- Microsoft certification with a Diploma in Computer Systems and Networks.

Experience

Miles Pty Ltd, Helpdesk/Desktop Support 3/9/10 – 21/12/13 (contract)
Technical environment

- Windows 7, MS Office 2010, Project 2010, SAP, McAfee, Visio 2010, Novell

Responsibilities

- Provide first level technical support to internal staff.
- Researched, resolved and responded to client queries and requests in a timely manner in accordance with established standards.
- Recorded and logged customer calls into the help desk system (approximately 30–70 per day).
- Resolved technical problems over the phone and provided desktop support on-site for more complex issues.
- Reset SAP, Windows 7 and Novell passwords as required.
- Basic Netware System Administration (changed permissions, modified groups and login scripts, modified user space limits).
- Set up and maintained HP network printers (changed toners, fusers and filters when required).
- Configured and maintained Dell Workstations and Laptops and patched network ports and switch set ups.
- Organised the repair of PCs and printers.

(1 of 3)

Joe Bowles

Continued...

Achievements
- Increased by 50% the number of first call resolutions.
- Awarded 'Employee of the Month' for exceptional client service, October 2013.
- Highest number of client commendations in Q2 and Q3 2011, Q1 2012 and Q1 2013.

Computer Power (A division of Reach Pty), 2nd Level Helpdesk 16/01/10 – 31/8/10 (contract)
Technical environment
- Windows XP, MS Office 2003
  Link Financial Management Software v 1.93 & v 2.0

Responsibilities
- Researched, resolved and responded to questions in a timely manner in accordance with established standards.
- Provided 2nd level phone support to clients and resolved escalated issues.
- Ensured data in the Financial Management System was accessible for all clients to use.

Insight Group, Desktop Support 23/02/06 – 12/12/09 (contract)
Technical environment
- MS Exchange 5.5, Exchange Client, Schedule +, Outlook 2003, Windows NT 5.2, Windows XP, MS SMS, Norton Ghost, Heat Call Logging Software, Citrix Metaframe

Responsibilities
- Coordinated the Email Support queue. This involved providing email support via the Helpdesk to 9000 users. Responsible for resolving the problem (usually 80%) or liaising with the other Exchange Administrator for the resolution of the remaining problems.
- Built and re-imaged pc/laptops as required.
- Used SMS to assist clients off site.
- Installed and configured external SCSI hard disk drive for the server.
- Patched new network and phone connections.
- Set up Compaq IPAQ (PDA) equipment for LAN access and remote access for mail and internet use.

Joe Bowles

Continued...

Responsibilities
- Installed and configured new software as required.
- Provided Desktop Support in all areas of Deakin Australia, including for the Directors and CEO.

Jones IT, MS Exchange (Email) Administrator 11/11/05 – 8/01/06 (3-month fixed term contract)
Technical environment
- MS Exchange 5.5, Outlook 2000/03, Windows NT 5.1, MS Office 2000/2003

Responsibilities
- Maintained the MS Exchange Environment and email queue.
- Created Mailboxes and Distribution Lists.
- Created Resource Mailboxes, conference rooms (set up to automatically reject or accept bookings).
- Conducted mail migration for clients.
- Provided 2nd/3rd level Email Support for the Helpdesk and managed unresolved calls.
- Helped maintain Public Folders.
- Monitored the WAN traffic and Exchange server integrity.

Overseas travel 7/01/05 – 10/10/05

Education & Training
Professional
- Microsoft Office Specialist (Master) certification
- MCITP Enterprise Desktop Support Technician (Skills Soft course)
- MCITP Windows 7 Enterprise Desktop Administrator (Skills Soft course)
- Microsoft Certified Professional (MCP)
- Network Essentials

Tertiary
- Diploma in Computer Systems and Networks   2004
  RMIT University — Melbourne, Australia

Memberships
- Member — Australian Computer Society (ACS)

Interests
- Squash
- Running a home network
- Playing computer games

(3 of 3)

Source: Pivotal HR www.pivotalhr.com.au (with adaptations).

Administration Professional (Temporary Contractor)

Lucy McLean
12 Maxwell Street
Christchurch NZ
02738 xxxxx
lucy.mclean@telecom.nz.co

Career Profile

Offering extensive administration experience and full-time availability to a temporary position in the corporate sector, government, tertiary or Rebuild sector in Christchurch, I have worked successfully for employers on a temporary basis since July 2012. Prior to this, I was a staff member at Christchurch Polytechnic Institute of Technology.

Key transferable skills:

- **Microsoft Office 2010:** Advanced Word, Excel, PowerPoint, Outlook, excellent document production
- **Data administration:** Excel, Access, PeopleSoft, TRIM, Aconex
- **Office and administrative management:** Facilities management, IT requirements, direct reports/team meetings, assets, purchasing, approvals
- **Personal assistant:** Calendar/email management, confidentiality, meeting/minutes coordination
- **Travel and finance:** Domestic and international bookings, budget and finance administration
- **Health & Safety:** Safety equipment, emergency evacuations, compliance and risk management
- **Human resource management:** Inductions, employment agreements, leave, change management, conflict resolution, employment relations

Employment History

Company Name: ABC Company   **15 October 2012 – 23 May 2013**

Title: Office/Administration Manager, temporary contract
ABC Company is a construction and insurance company within the Christchurch Rebuild. I undertook the role of Office/Administration Manager due to illness of the permanent employee. I quickly became familiar with a busy role, and expanded the position to fully function as Personal Assistant to the Joint Venture Management Team within six weeks as a temporary employee.

Responsibilities:

- Calendar and email management.
- Minute-taking for management meetings and program services meetings.
- Communications with domestic and commercial project teams.
- Provided administrative support and events coordination for the Communications Manager.
- Health & Safety, vehicle and safety equipment coordination.
- Undertook office reconfiguration for contact centre.

(1 of 3)

Career Profile   **Lucy McLean**

Company Name: X Company   **16 July 2012 – 14 September 2012**

Title: Human Resource Administrator, temporary contract
Assisted the X Company's human resources team for two months, with the objective
of reducing their administrative burden. I enjoyed a smooth transition into the team at
X Company, where the HR, ICT, Customer Services, Resource Management and Compliance
teams worked together closely.

Responsibilities:

* Typed routine correspondence for the HR Manager.
* Assisted HR Advisors with remuneration review and recruitment requirements. This included
  arranging interviews, communicating with applicants, reference checking and coordinating a
  full recruitment day at CBS arena for Consents Planner applicants in August 2012.
* Scanned and transferred HR documents into TRIM (document management system).

Company Name: Christchurch Polytechnic   **29 March 2010 – 15 June 2012**
Institute of Technology

Title: Academic Faculty Administrator
Academic faculty administrator receiving applications, meeting students, and providing
secretarial support to Academic Programme Leaders and Heads of Schools.
I provided administrative support to three academic schools, assisted Senior Nursing lecturers
and was a member of a large administration team.

Responsibilities:

* Provided assistance to the Head of the School of Architectural Studies, and the Programme
  Leader of Interior Design & Interior Décor.
* Handled travel, finance, research grants and Hui registrations and provided support to the
  Team Leader, Nursing Placements, and the Nursing and Midwifery lecturers.
* Arranged nursing student accommodation, including booking accommodation for groups of
  students on nursing placements.
* Processed applications and enrolments.
* Managed faculty finance administration.
* Prepared staff reimbursements and credit card reconciliations.
* Assisted with purchasing requirements, including raising purchase orders, dealing with
  suppliers and completing vendor processes.
* Organised travel, accommodation, cars and conference bookings for academic staff and
  visiting academics.
* Produced documents and organised document management.

Company Name: Christchurch Polytechnic   **7 April 2008 – 19 March 2010**
Institute of Technology

Title: Senior Administrator
A permanent senior administrator position that provided support to the Director of ICT, and
ICT teams servicing the information and technological needs of the Polytechnic. The position
also included secretarial support to the Project Governance Group, led by the Chief Financial
Officer.

Career Profile   **Lucy McLean**

Continued...

Responsibilities:

- Formatted and prepared tenders for submission and assisted with tender communications.
- Managed phone accounts across the business, and liaised with telecommunications providers regarding outstanding accounts.
- Arranged, recorded and distributed meeting minutes.
- Facilitated office configurations, controlled purchasing and managed invoicing.
- Organised events on behalf of the ICT Director, including external events for ICT stakeholders.

Education and Training

Christchurch Polytechnic Institute of Technology, 2008 – 2012

Introduction to Business Analysis
Employment Relations
InDesign
Microsoft Access

Employment Law Training, Christchurch, 2003

Pay and Personnel Administration

Macquarie University NSW (external), 2001

Certificate in Superannuation – Theory and Practice

Curtin University of Technology Perth, 1997 – 2002

Bachelor of Science

- Psychology
- Human Resource Management
- Research Methods/data analysis
- Management
- Planetary Science
- Volunteer in Psych Student Resource Centre

Referees
Name
Title
Company
DDI: 000
Email: xxx

(3 of 3)

Source: From the authors.

Chapter 11

Resumes for School Leavers

So you're done with school and keen to join the paid workforce armed with enthusiasm and a willingness to take on a different kind of learning. From here on out you'll develop yourself through employer training, watching colleagues, trying things yourself and asking questions. However, first you have to land the job.

Your resume is like a sales brochure showcasing all the wonderful features of this fantastic product — you! Your resume remains your marketing brochure no matter how old you get, but when you're a school leaver, your sales pitch is a lot different to when you have years of work experience under your belt. Never fear. The workforce needs people like you.

In this chapter, we cover what to include in your resume, how long it should be and how to avoid getting yourself binned before you've even made it to the job interview, whether you're looking for a full-time job to plant your foot on that first rung of the career ladder or you just want to earn yourself some extra cash while at university or college.

Exploring Your Employability

Recruiters and employers know you don't have lots of work experience. They are more focused on hiring on *potential* — your potential to fit into the organisation and do a good job.

They assess your potential based on a set of basic employability skills that combine 'hard' skills such as literacy with 'soft' skills such as your ability to get on with others. Employers are also looking for people who demonstrate respectful behaviours, such as turning up on time, being well groomed and even being a good listener.

Whether you're looking on an employment information site such as Careers New Zealand or reading media interviews with employers such as the Australian Industry Group (or even quizzing the employers and managers in your family!), the top skills valued by employers are pretty much the same. The demand for these skills is high but the good news is acquiring such skills is within the grasp of school leavers — you may even find that you've already got some of them. Ready to hear what they are? Okay, here are the top five:

- ✔ Literacy and numeracy skills

- ✔ Communication skills

- ✔ IT skills — or, at least, confidence using computers

- ✔ Ability to work in a team

- ✔ Customer service skills

Your literacy and numeracy skills relate to subjects such as English and maths. Your communication skills relate to how well you listen and then interact with others. Examples of where you may have developed these skills include making verbal presentations in class, or being a member of the debating team. IT skills include everything from using a computer at school to uploading content to your social media sites. Examples of teamwork could include sporting teams, community and volunteer work or working on a group school project.

You may be thinking, Customer service skills? I haven't even had a full-time job yet! Think harder. Have you had a part-time job babysitting or working in a café or retail store? Have you worked on a stall at a fete or performed yard work for neighbours? If so, you have acquired customer service skills.

Use the list of the top five in-demand skills to identify your employability skills and then write them down. Ask a family member or friend to help prompt you if you find you're struggling to pinpoint the skills you have and where you acquired them.

If you have completed a Vocational Education and Training (VET) qualification, look out for employability skills identified within units of competency. A full listing of all VET training packages and employability skills can be found at www.training.gov.au.

Employers know what to look for in a school leaver resume. You may think nothing of your role adding up the takings from the footie club sausage sizzle; however, an employer would see that as cash handling experience and performing a role of trust and responsibility — both great for a retail job. A part-time job will be viewed as you having experience forming a work habit — turning up on time, following instructions from a manager and having to dress and act a certain way. All experience is good experience.

Selling Your Skills in a School Leaver Resume

In the preceding section we cover what employers are looking for in a school leaver employee. Now, we cover what information to include in your resume and where to place it.

The good news is that your resume only needs to be a page long — two at the most. The challenging news is that you need to tailor your resume to each job you're going for to play up your strengths. A resume for a job as a waitress in your local cafe is going to be different from one you would send to an accounting firm to apply for a summer job while you study for a bachelor of business degree majoring in accounting. For the waitressing job, you would focus on any customer service experience you have, as well as your people skills. To land the summer job, you would highlight your academic results in related subjects, as well as include your plans to study accounting at university.

The following is a list of the basic elements of a school leaver resume:

- Your name and contact information
- Career objective (optional, depending on the job)
- Key skills (a brief list)
- Education

- Work history
- Referees

You can tailor pretty much every one of these elements (except your contact details) for different jobs.

Keeping the format simple

A resume is different to the type of marketing documents that rely on exaggerated statements and colourful images to attract attention. Fancy, fun and fabulous just doesn't work when job hunting. Keeping your resume real as well as real simple is the way to go.

Start by using an easy-to-read font such as 11 point Arial or Times New Roman. No need for fancy fonts, photos, graphics or colours. Your candidate story is compelling enough, and keeping the layout simple will ensure a recruiter or employer can quickly spot the information needed to make a favourable decision about you.

For more tips on keeping it simple to keep the recruiter's attention, read the section, 'How to Lose a Job in 30 Seconds' at the end of this chapter.

We have contact

Your resume should start with your name and contact details, namely your phone number and email address. Sounds easy, right? Well, it's the little things that matter most here, and attention to these details will help keep your resume in the running:

- Check that your email address uses your name — and we don't mean your nickname. `Emily.Brown@telecom.co.nz` sounds so much better than `Bossypants@telecom.co.nz`.
- If you've only got a fun and funky email address, create a new one for use while job hunting.
- Include your mobile phone number if you have one, but remember to check your voicemail message first to ensure you're speaking clearly, slowly and politely when inviting the caller to leave a message.

✔ Make sure you use your full name in your voicemail message (not just your first name). This will help the employer get a handle on the correct pronunciation to use if you have an unusual name — but that will only happen if you speak slowly and clearly.

✔ Use the *generational test*; in other words, ask Mum, Dad or an aunty or uncle to listen to and review your message. If you don't have a mobile number, re-record the family landline voicemail message to make sure it's clear and tells the caller that they have reached the 'Gonzales household' — using your own family name of course!

For more advice on presenting your contact details in your resume, refer to Chapter 3.

Crafting your career objective

A *career objective* tells an employer about your career ambition or goal in just a sentence or two. You would only use a career objective for career-related roles, such as that entry-level job in a large organisation that you hope will lead to bigger things, or that summer job in the profession or industry you hope to join when you finish university.

Start the first sentence of your career objective with a word other than 'I'. For example, if you were applying for a summer job in an accounting firm, you'd write something like:

Career Objective

A high school graduate soon to start an accounting degree, my ultimate goal is to become a chartered accountant in an established firm.

If you're applying for a weekend job at a pet-grooming salon, the career objective is unnecessary. As you're trying to keep your resume to a page or two, don't include this element unless it will boost your chances of getting the job.

Presenting your key skills

An employer receives a number of job applications for any one role advertised, so will spend about 30 seconds 'scanning' rather than reading each resume — at least the first time around. For this reason, grabbing the recruiter's attention quickly is essential.

The resumes of older job candidates often include a list of key skills as the first or second item after their name and contact details, as a way of saying 'over here, pick me'. In such cases, the candidate reads the job ad carefully, underlining the words used by the employer to describe the skills the successful candidate should have. These words can then be used in their key skills list.

Using the five employability skills we referred to in the earlier section 'Exploring your Employability', you could do the same to grab the employer's attention. See the following example, and note how brief we have been.

> Emily Brown
>
> 14 Thompson Street, Queenstown
>
> M: 027385166 E: Emily.Brown@telecom.co.nz

Key Skills

- ✔ High-level literacy and numeracy skills, demonstrated by my grades in English and maths
- ✔ Good communication skills developed through my membership in public speaking club Toastmasters
- ✔ Excellent IT skills, including Microsoft Office, content management and publishing tools, plus experience using a range of social media platforms
- ✔ Teamwork and customer service experience gained through team sports and part-time work at McDonald's

Explore these skills in more detail in the appropriate section of your resume. For example, share your English and maths results — if they are good — under the heading 'Education', and outline the particulars of the part-time role at McDonald's under the heading 'Work History'. The details of any team sports are placed under the heading 'Hobbies and Interests' or 'Extracurricular Activities'.

Refer to Chapter 3 for more guidance on including a key skills list in your resume.

Showing off your academic achievements

Time to play up your smarts and play down any areas of weakness. You can use the heading 'Education' or choose a heading such as 'Educational Achievements' to showcase marks and prizes when applying for that top job, or 'Education and Training' if you've completed a vocational program and want to highlight any certificates you've obtained, or a level achieved on a trade course.

Include only the relevant subjects for the job in question, although maths and English always rate highly with employers. For example, if you're applying for a job as a retail assistant in a shop selling science toys and puzzles, include your science subjects. You can either list each subject with a mark beside it or provide a summary if your marks are either not relevant or not so flash.

In this example, Mat doesn't attract attention to his individual marks, only his overall mark:

Mathew Chan

44 Fort Street, Hamilton, Brisbane, Qld 4007.
Mobile: 0408 xxxx

Education

Brisbane Grammar School, Years 6 – 12, completed in 2013

Overall Position (OP): 6 (English, Mathematics, Economics, Earth Sciences, Modern History).

Here, the candidate draws attention to his level of achievement in each subject:

Mathew Chan

44 Fort Street, Hamilton, Brisbane, Qld 4007.
Mobile: 0408 xxxx

Education

Brisbane Grammar School, Years 6 – 12, completed in 2013

Overall Position (OP): 6

- **English**   Very High Achievement
- **Mathematics** Very High Achievement
- **Economics**   Very High Achievement

If you really want to make your school achievements pop, use a heading and a dot point list to catch an employer's eye.

Academic Achievements
- Year 12 artwork shortlisted for HSC Art Express Exhibition
- Received a scholarship to the Gunter Institute to study German
- Won silver medal in the Biology Australian Science Olympiad Exam
- Achieved High Distinctions for English and Math
- Certificate of Distinction for Australian National Chemistry Quiz

Highlighting vocational training

If you've completed vocational training through a school program, list your qualifications starting with the most recently obtained, and then work backwards in time.

There are so many wonderful courses available through vocational programs in schools. Such qualifications are highly regarded by employers, so if you were a top performer your resume is the place to show off marks, prizes and accolades. You can use a heading such as 'Achievements' to list prizes and outstanding results.

Sharing your work history

These days, many school students gain some sort of work experience during their study years. This could include formal work such as a part-time job or informal, casual or volunteer work. Whether you've been a DJ at a community event, provided babysitting services in the neighbourhood, tutored other school students or helped out at a charity event, you've acquired valuable experience that an employer wants to know about. Many young people today are also starting their own businesses, and such ventures should also be included. Briefly list the responsibilities you carried out in each job, and also list any achievements for each job such as a staff award, a promotion or an outstanding sales or customer service result. See Figure 11-1 for an example of how to present your work history in your resume.

12/55 Davison Street, Parramatta, NSW 2150
E: Charles.Abed@provider.com.au M: 0414 xxxxxx

Work History
Shift manager, (Part-time hours), Magic Family Restaurant in Church Street, Parramatta

May 2012 – Current

Responsibilities: Manage staff, document supplies that need re-ordering, greet suppliers and supervise unloading and restocking, deal with customers, cash handling and banking.

Achievements:
- Named Staff Member of the Year, 2012
- Received letters of thanks from a range of customers for outstanding customer service
- Suggestion of a new gluten-free menu adopted, resulting in a 10% increase in sales and new customers

Waiter, (Part-time hours), Magic Family Restaurant, Parramatta

November 2011 – April 2012

Responsibilities: Take customer orders and answer questions about menu items, relay orders to the kitchen, clear and reset tables.

Achievements:
- Praised by the owner for successfully turning around an irate customer, resulting in repeat business
- Promoted from team member to shift manager in April 2012

Owner, MatchCarSwap.com.au

March 2011 – current

Created an internet business where people can collect and swap match box cars.

Responsibilities: Finding and managing suppliers such as a web developer and a designer; moderating the blog on the site to ensure all comments are constructive; understanding spam and online laws and maintaining the website's high standards.

Achievements:
- Increased user traffic by 52% from 2012 to 2013 through a public relations campaign devised in-house
- Received consistent positive feedback from visitors
- Named a 'site to watch' by review site WebbyTales.com

*This candidate had a job and was running his own small web-based business simultaneously.

Figure 11-1: An example of how to lay out work history in a resume.*

We provide more information on presenting your work achievements in Chapter 3.

Introducing your added extras

While the goal is to keep your resume to only a page or two, if you have completed a training course or have a particular skill that you can put to work for an employer, sing out about it.

You can use a simple heading such as 'Additional Skills and Training'. Some examples include

- Barista training
- First aid certificate
- Driver's licence
- Leadership training
- Vocational certificates
- IT training and certifications

Revealing your hobbies and interests

You may wonder, 'Do employers really care about extracurricular activities, such as scouts, surf lifesaving or competitive sport?' If so, the answer is yes!

Including a 'Hobbies and Interests' or 'Extracurricular Activities' section serves a number of purposes, including

- Helping recruiters or employers get a better picture of you
- Backing up claims on your resume — such as demonstrating teamwork, for example, when listing a team sport
- Providing the recruiter or employer with information they can use to make conversation and put you at ease when they first meet you

Here are some examples of extracurricular activities you can list in your resume:

- School Fundraising Coordinator for [name of charity]
- Represented the school in netball at the district competition
- Elected school prefect for Years 11 and 12

Including hobbies and interests can sometimes undermine your job application. By including 'Facebook' as a hobby, an employer may mistakenly believe you're going to spend work time updating your status and reading comments from friends. Your hobby of stunt mountain-bike riding may leave a recruiter concerned that you'll take lots of sick days to nurse injuries.

Remembering your referees

'Referees' should appear as the last heading on your resume. Having at least two referees is a must, and if they're strong referees you don't need to list more. From an employer's point of view the most valuable referee is someone who has managed you directly, such as the owner of the cafe or manager of the store where you worked part-time. Other referees that may impress would be the parents who employed you to watch their children, the coach or manager of your sports team, your Scout or Guide leader or the person who manages the organisation where you volunteer.

Supply the contact details of more than two referees when you have only had one paid job. If you're applying for your first ever paid job, ensure your referees are people who have supervised you, such as a coach or teacher. Family members are not suitable referees, even when they have owned the business where you worked part-time. In such cases, ask another manager to vouch for you.

Recruiters and employers prefer to phone your referees and talk to them about their experience managing you rather than accept a written reference. If you want to include written references to support your application, go ahead but also point out that each referee can be contacted by phone.

Always ask someone if they will be your referee before applying for a job or supplying their name and contact details to a potential employer. Tell your referees a little about the role you have applied for and the key skills and attributes the employer wants applicants to have. Also ask their preferred mode of contact — although many recruiters will want a landline as well as a mobile phone number — and check the time of day that is most convenient for them to take a call on your behalf. This show of respect to both the referee and the recruiter or employer also earns you added points.

Going for Cover Letter Gold

You've created a resume that will position you as shortlist material . . . However, all your effort could go to waste without a cover letter that makes it clear to an employer why you're worth meeting. Your cover letter is your first opportunity to sell yourself. In most cases, employers read your cover letter before reading your resume: A rushed job could spell a lost opportunity.

Don't undo all your hard work by coupling a sparking resume with a lacklustre cover letter. Instead, create a calling card that makes employers sit up and take notice.

The magic formula for cover letters is simple:

- ✔ **Keep it short.** Three to four paragraphs will do.

- ✔ **Stay relevant.** Make sure the information is relevant to the specific job you're applying for.

- ✔ **Be truthful.** Everything you state must be truthful and easy for you to back up when you meet the employer in person.

- ✔ **Explain yourself effectively.** Your pitch for the job must be compelling and well written, with no typos or grammatical errors.

Note that your name and contact details must appear at the top of the letter. Try to find a real person to address the letter to and include the person's title plus the date. The cover letter must attract immediate attention and also serve as a positive example of your literacy skills and enthusiasm.

We go into more detail about cover letters in Chapter 7, but Figures 11-2 and 11-3 introduce you to some specific ideas on how you might introduce yourself as a school leaver looking to enter the world of work.

In Figure 11-2, Jodie is applying for a role in a retail store she knows well, and that fits with her VET qualification and informal work experience.

In Figure 11-3, Jake is applying for a casual job, but he has no relevant experience. Note that he is highlighting his keenness and initiative by visiting the employer's place of business first, finding out the name of the person he should apply to and flagging his availability. Our applicant has also played up his personal attributes.

Jodie Myers
280 Bobbin Head Road
North Turramurra NSW 2074
Email: jmyers@provider.com.au
M: 0438 xxx xxx

22 January 2014

Ms Wendy Chan
Manager, Call of the Wild

Dear Ms Chan

I am writing to apply for the position of customer consultant in your pet mega store advertised in this week's *North Shore Times* newspaper.

A regular visitor to your store, I admire the way your staff are so friendly and have such great product knowledge when assisting customers. I have also heard you offer a good training program to new recruits.

Please find my resume attached; of particular relevance is my Certificate II in Retail Operations (sales assistants) and my work experience at the Keith Sullivan Newsagency and a holiday job at the North Turramurra Veterinary Hospital.

I believe my qualification and experience, plus the fact I have my own transport, a current driver's licence and referees who know my strong record of reliability and punctuality, make me well suited to your role.

Yours sincerely

Jodie Myers

Figure 11-2: An example cover letter for a school leaver applying for a retail job.

Jake Miller
2/27 Blondell Avenue
Budds Beach
Surfers Paradise QLD 4217
Email: jake.miller@bigpond.com
0402 xxx xxx

18 February 2014

Mr Toby Brown
Owner, McDonald's Family Restaurant
Niecon Plaza
Broadbeach QLD 4218

Dear Mr Brown

Wendy Mobowie, Assistant Manager, suggested I contact you regarding casual Crew Member positions in your McDonald's Restaurant in Niecon Plaza. She mentioned that you are currently hiring new staff and there may be a possibility to come in and speak to you over the next two weeks.

I am currently a Year 10 school leaver with a range of expertise, including working as a surf instructor on Main Beach. I am a hard worker, quick learner and can handle pressure. I am interested in working for McDonald's because I would like to gain more experience in customer service and retail. I also find it easy to get on with people and enjoy being part of a team. I feel your organisation would be a great place to work because it is successful, has high standards of service and great food.

I am available for an interview any time and look forward to speaking with you in person in the next week or so.

Yours sincerely

Jake Miller

Figure 11-3: An example of a cover letter for a school leaver applying for a casual job when he has no relevant experience.

How to Lose a Job in 30 Seconds

Recruiters and employers are time-poor, so if something about your resume raises a red flag, don't expect a phone call or email asking you what's up. Your resume will be binned in favour of the next candidate. As the old saying goes, 'You never get a second chance to make a first impression', so don't rush your resume.

Here are some things to look out for to ensure you don't blow your chances in the 30 seconds or so a recruiter or employer takes to gain their first impression of you:

- **Use a second pair of eyes:** Be sure you have produced a document that is free of spelling and grammatical errors. Once you have read and re-read your resume, ask a family member or teacher to review it for you.

- **Don't exaggerate or 'create' facts:** You are new at this employment game, but the person you have submitted your application to is not. If you create a lofty job title for yourself, make up a job or create responsibilities you've never held or achievements you've never earned, you will be found out.

- **Email with respect:** Most job applications are emailed these days, so check you have attached your resume and any certifications or supporting documents asked for. Use the subject line to state your name and the obvious: 'Application for the office assistant role at XYZ Company'. Err on the side of respectful caution and use 'Ms', 'Miss', 'Mrs' or 'Mr' when addressing the recruiter or employer. Also construct a polite message to go in the body of the email, such as 'Dear Mr Yagan, I am applying for the role of office manager. Please find attached a copy of my resume for your consideration. Yours sincerely [your name].'

- **Be social media savvy:** Many recruiters and employers will search your name online via Google or Bing before they meet you. Apply the maximum security settings to your Facebook profile before you start job hunting. Also perform your own online searches using your name and remove any images or comments that present you in a negative light, and dress up any online features that you want found. For example, if you have a blog, make sure no spelling errors appear in your last few posts.

Chapter 12

Graduating to the World of Work — Resumes for Graduates

*N*o more cramming for exams, plugging away at assignments or attending lectures ... time to get a job.

Whether you're applying for a place on a graduate recruitment program or your first 'career' job, most employers and recruiters will look beyond your academic record when assessing if you are the best person for their job. Employers want well-rounded grad recruits who have good interpersonal and social skills as well as relevant academic credentials.

Some jobs will always make academic grades one of the key prerequisites, but for many roles the fact you did not score in the top 10 per cent of your degree program is not a barrier to employment.

Any work experience you have — even when not industry-related — is valued by employers. Extracurricular activities also speak volumes about your aptitude for responsibility, and even leadership. So, if you've been captain of a sporting team, a member of a university committee or have taken part in volunteer work for a charity, we show you how to include this detail on your resume.

In this chapter, we also look at graduate recruitment programs, and offer you some online resources to help you get a head start in your career.

Reckoning on Recruitment Programs for Grads

Each year a number of lucky graduates are accepted into these programs in both the private and public sectors. The size of the intake depends on broader economic conditions. In good times, companies take on more graduates, while in challenging times, they cut back on places. *Graduate recruitment programs* are structured development programs that run for 12 months or more, incorporating on-the-job work experience by rotating graduates through a number of departments within the organisation, exposing them to all facets of the business.

If you want to get into a graduate recruitment program, look for jobs posted on company websites, visit university career sites and career fairs, attend employer-hosted open days and talk to the career counsellors on campus. Also, use the list of useful websites for graduates provided at the end of this chapter.

Presenting Information in a Graduate Resume

Throughout this section we provide graduates with guidance on what to include in their resume and how to structure that information. To get started, use these headings as a guide:

- ✔ Contact information
- ✔ Career objective (optional)
- ✔ Education/academic achievements
- ✔ Work experience/achievements
- ✔ Key skills/competency statements (optional)
- ✔ Extracurricular activities
- ✔ Additional skills (IT skills, languages)

- ✔ Interests
- ✔ Professional development
- ✔ Memberships
- ✔ Referees

Staying in contact

When it comes to securing a job, you need to be easy to contact. Make sure your contact details are clearly laid out on the front page of your resume — they need to jump out at a recruiter.

Keep these points in mind when deciding on the contact details to include on your resume:

- ✔ **Mobile number:** Sure, list your mobile number, but if you do, don't forget to check your voicemail and text messages regularly. Employers and recruiters will often try to reach you on your phone, and you need to ensure you respond promptly.

- ✔ **Alternative contact:** List more than one contact number in your resume if you can (this increases the odds of the recruiter being able to reach you).

- ✔ **Email etiquette:** Know the capacity limits of the email provider you use and clear old messages regularly to ensure important messages from employers and recruiters get through. Also, use a version of your name in your email address. A fun or funky email address could get your resume binned.

- ✔ **Voicemail:** Re-record your voicemail message to sound as business-like as possible. Speak slowly and clearly. And don't forget to check for messages regularly.

Focusing on career objectives

A *career objective* is a short statement or paragraph at the beginning of your resume that tells the reader about your career goals and aspirations. Including a career objective is not mandatory, but it can provide an employer with greater insight into where you may fit into their organisation over the long term. If you decide to include a career objective in your resume, tailor the information to the graduate program or job role you're going for rather than use a one-size-fits-all approach.

Keep your career objective simple, clear and to the point. We provide more detail on career objectives in Chapter 3.

Making the grade

The first information to list — after your contact details — is your educational qualifications under a heading such as 'Education' or 'Educational Qualifications'. If your tertiary entrance results and university grades were impressive (credit level or higher), highlight them underneath your qualifications as shown here. You can include details from your secondary school years too if impressive. Employers appreciate top-class performers with a history of solid academic performance.

Education

Bachelor of Multimedia

Griffith University, Nathan (2013)

Grade Point Average: 6.5 (Scale 1–7, 7 highest)

Higher School Certificate

Sydney Boys High School (2010)

Universities Admission Index: 91.7

If your tertiary entrance grades or university results are far from glowing, list only your degree rather than your specific results. Include only the subjects or course units from secondary school you did well in and list the qualification achieved. Here is an example:

Western Australian Certificate of Education, Rossmoyne Senior High School (2013)

Economics   B

German   B

Don't bother spelling out all your subjects, course codes and marks; instead, attach to your application a copy of your academic transcript or statement of results. Only put in subjects and results you want to draw attention to.

If you're applying for graduate programs in advance and are in the throes of completing a degree, mention in your educational qualifications section the name of your qualification, the institution you're attending, any majors and expected year of completion. Here's an example:

Bachelor of Engineering

The Australian National University (expected year of completion 2015)

Showing off your academic achievements

After your education details, list your academic achievements (if any) under a heading such as 'Academic Achievements'. Make the recruiter want to meet you by flaunting any major successes, or noteworthy awards and prizes. For example:

Academic Achievements

Received a written letter of commendation from the University Chancellor for outstanding academic performance

Top 5% of students to graduate with first class honours

[Name of university] University Medal (faculty)

Admitted onto the Dean's Merit List

Achieved a Grade Point Average of 6.2

Outstanding academic achievement with 15 high distinctions, 5 distinctions and 4 credits for subjects completed

Awarded [name of prize] for attaining the highest aggregate mark in [name of subject]

Free resume services

Resume help is readily available at your university or school career centre. The good news is that you won't be out of pocket, because these services are free. Universities and schools offer a range of resume services, including:

✓ Careers counsellors or career advisers who can review your resume and offer resume advice

✓ Short seminars or workshops to develop your resume writing skills

✓ The latest career info, such as books, website references and dates for career fairs

Weighing up your work experience

Landing a 'real' job fresh from uni is competitive and not every grad has relevant industry-related work experience under their belt. The good news is that employers value all work experience, including that part-time job, casual work experience or volunteer role you held. Work experience can include the following:

- ✔ **Holiday work/work experience:** List any unpaid work experience you've done while studying. Nail that job by drawing attention to the fact that you've got some real-life work experience and training in your chosen field.

- ✔ **Part-time or casual jobs:** If you've had no industry jobs, include any work experience you've undertaken to make ends meet while at uni or school. Starting out at the checkout of a supermarket, serving up burgers and fries or waiting on tables on weekends gives you a host of valuable work-related skills — customer service, teamwork, time management, problem solving, flexibility . . . the list goes on. This type of experience shows the recruiter you can handle more than just studying and are capable of dealing with the public.

- ✔ **Temporary jobs through agencies:** Note down any stints of temporary work sourced through recruitment agencies.

- ✔ **Voluntary work:** Add in any volunteer, community or charity-based work.

Group all your experience together under the heading 'Work Experience' or 'Employment History', listing your most recent job first, going backwards. Alternatively, you can split your career-related and unrelated work experience into two categories — 'Professional Experience' and 'Other Experience' as shown in Figure 12-1. Don't forget to add in a few achievements too! For more information on presenting your work achievements, refer to Chapter 3.

PROFESSIONAL EXPERIENCE

Summer Vacation Program   December 2012 – February 2013
Cooper & Wallace Accountants (Melbourne)

Audit Division
- Participated in a five-day induction program covering company procedures and policies, professional grooming, business etiquette and relationship building.
- Accompanied senior auditors on client visits.
- Attended compulsory audit training.
- Reconciled invoices and checked journal entries.
- Assisted in the preparation of audit reports.
- Maintained an efficient records management system.
- Interviewed clients to gather information on their operating procedures and accounts.
- Participated in professional development activities, networking functions and corporate events.
- Shadowed a 'buddy' for a day.
- Completed other duties as assigned.

OTHER EXPERIENCE

Casual Sales Assistant   December 2011 – Present
Flaunt-it Fashions (Melbourne)

- Opened and closed the store on weekends.
- Processed cash, cheque and credit card transactions in a prompt and professional manner.
- Merchandised, ordered, priced and maintained stock levels.
- Supervised and trained new staff in store procedures.
- Prepared a weekly staff roster.
- Participated in annual stock takes.
- Maintained the cleanliness of the store.

Achievements
- Won 'Casual of the Year' award for highest sales in 2013.
- Increased sales by 20% through creative merchandising and cross-selling products to customers.

Figure 12-1: Detailing your work experience.

Listing your key skills and writing competency statements

Competency statements usually appear before or after the work experience section on a resume. They're short paragraphs of text that demonstrate to a potential employer your skills, abilities, knowledge and personal attributes. Competency statements can be linked to the job. For example, if the job ad mentions strong communication skills, list communication skills as one of your competency statements. If you're a graduate with limited experience, competency statements can be a good way to draw attention to transferable skills gained through study, work experience or extracurricular activities.

According to Jim Bright, author of *Job Hunting For Dummies*, 2nd Edition (published by Wiley), competency statements are made up of the following three components:

- ✔ **A snappy title:** The words you use should summarise your positive qualities, preferably using the jargon in the job ad.

- ✔ **A statement of fit:** This statement takes the shape of a sentence or two explaining that you possess the necessary qualities for the job.

- ✔ **Evidence:** The recruiter should be able to double-check the contents of your statement by referring to your qualification or the referees listed in your resume.

Using this framework as a guide, here's an example to illustrate:

Computing Skills

I am skilled in using a variety of computing packages and learn new applications quickly. I use Microsoft Word to type my assignments and Microsoft PowerPoint to create group presentations. In one of my subjects, Understanding Data, I created charts, used formulas and presented statistical information in tables using Microsoft Excel [statement of fit]. Recently, I was computer tested in Word, Excel and PowerPoint at XYZ Recruitment Agency. Test results reveal I have advanced proficiency in all three packages, with a current typing speed of 80 wpm with 92% accuracy. A copy of the test results is available upon request [evidence].

How employable are you?

In 2001, the Australian Chamber of Commerce and Industry (ACCI) and the Business Council of Australia (BCA), produced a report detailing a list of employability skills needed by industry. The *Employability Skills for the Future* project identified eight key skills noted by employers as critical to employability. The key skills in demand are: Communication, teamwork, problem-solving, initiative and enterprise, planning and organising, self-management, learning, and technology.

Using this list, identify the skills you already possess and look for ways to include these on your resume in your Responsibilities and Achievements sections. If you're struggling to identify these employability skills in your life experience to date, look for ways to acquire new skills through part-time employment, study, work experience, sporting activities, community work and so on. Many universities run employability skills workshops for students. Employability skills are also incorporated into Vocational Education and Training (VET) courses (see www .training.gov.au).

Noting your noteworthy achievements

Don't despair if you're lacking in work experience. You can supplement your shortcomings by playing up any extracurricular activities, such as sports, community and social activities. These show that you're a well-rounded individual with a range of interests and skills, such as perseverance, initiative, organisational skills and leadership. The key is to list the added extras that show you're a motivated, energetic member of your community.

Extracurricular activities can include

- ✔ **Community or volunteer work.** For example, volunteer roles, fundraising or coordinating of a charity event.

- ✔ **Membership of industry associations, groups or clubs.** For example, a committee member of an accounting students association, member of a drama society, chairman of a university or college debating team, or member of a church group.

✔ **Sporting interests and achievements.** For example, being captain of a sporting team, secretary or treasurer of a community group or team manager for a particular sport in the university games.

✔ **Travel.** For example, if you travelled to a particular country to participate in a charity program.

✔ **University or campus activities.** For example, being activities officer of a university student association, secretary of the student union, editor of a university publication, a member of a sports team, participant in the buddy program for international students, or volunteer for orientation week.

You can group your extracurricular activities under one heading or combine your extracurricular activities with your achievements. Following are two different ways to present extracurricular activities in your resume.

Group your activities under one heading:

University/Community Involvement

2013	Club Executive for the Creative Industry Associations
2012	President of the Musical Society
2012	Member of Toastmasters International
2011	Lead role in the school musical 'Oliver'

Focus on detailing your achievements:

Achievements

2013   President, QUT Student Guild

Increased membership from 4,500 to 8000 within a year through awareness campaigns and membership events on campus.

2012   Education Officer, QUT Engineers Without Borders

Organised a networking seminar for engineering students with guest speakers from government and the private sector.

2012   Committee Member, Young Engineers
        Australia (QLD)

        Part of the team that organised a Gala Ball.

        Interacted with VIPs including Ministers and other
        government officials at Technical Forums.

Adding additional skills

List any additional skills you have, such as the fact that you
have used content management systems to maintain a website
or that you are fluent in a foreign language.

Including personal interests

Give the recruiter or employer a feel for who you are by
including personal interests in your resume, using a heading
such as 'Hobbies and Interests' or just 'Personal Interests'.
Having a particular interest could also align with the job
role. For example, an employer from a start-up company may
appreciate the risk-taking qualities of someone involved in
adventure sports. Having a range of interests shows that you're
a well-rounded person.

Covering professional development

Add in any training or short courses you attended under the
heading 'Professional Development'. Include the name of the
course, the provider and year completed. We provide more
information on this in Chapter 3.

Mentioning professional memberships

Many associations offer either free or low-cost membership
to university students and graduates. Using the heading
'Memberships', list any industry groups or associations you
have joined. This shows you're committed and interested in
professional development.

Referees who count

Include the names of two to three referees in your resume who will vouch for you and your abilities. Be sure to ask permission beforehand and don't use friends or relatives.

Suitable referees include

✔ Work supervisor/manager at your part-time, casual, holiday or temp job

✔ Agency recruitment consultant (temp job through an agency)

✔ Community/volunteer supervisor

✔ Lecturer at university, or thesis supervisor

For more information on how to present your referees, refer to Chapter 3.

Creating a First-Class Cover Letter

Now you have all the information needed to create an outstanding resume (refer to preceding sections), it's time to write the perfect cover letter to ensure your masterpiece of self-promotion gets read.

You want to excite the recruiter or employer in just three or four paragraphs by demonstrating you have the backstory they're searching for. You only get a few seconds to create the right impression, so be selective about the information you share. The cover letter is not a summary of your resume but a strategic glimpse. The employer or recruiter's job ad will spell out the education, personal attributes and experience required to get shortlisted for interview, so pay close attention to these requirements to make sure you're ticking all the right boxes.

We share many more tips about cover letter writing in Chapter 7, but here are a few important things for graduates to keep in mind when writing a cover letter:

✔ The main job of your cover letter is to ensure your resume gets read.

✔ Every sentence should position you as the right person for the job.

✔ Your cover letter is the first opportunity to demonstrate that you are articulate and pay close attention to detail. Make sure your cover letter is error-free — check it has no misspellings and that you use the right company name.

✔ Use a reference number or mention where you saw the job ad.

✔ Your cover letter must sing with enthusiasm. Sell the relevancy of your education, skills and experience to the job on offer.

✔ Your contact details are part of your sales pitch, so no funky email moniker. Also, ensure you have a voicemail service when including a mobile number. Be easy to reach.

✔ Addressing your cover letter to a real person is better than using a general title like 'Dear Sir/Madam', so do your homework.

✔ Always lean on the side of formality. Refer to the recruitment consultant or employment managers by using 'Mr/Mrs/Miss' and so on, rather than calling them by their first name.

To help you get started, we have included two sample cover letters for inspiration. In the first example (Figure 12-2), Robert is trying to score a place in a prestigious law firm's two-year graduate program. His research has found that the firm prefers candidates of high academic achievement holding double degrees. The firm's website also mentions a preference for employees with languages and a strong interest in global business.

In the second example (Figure 12-3), Lucy is trying to score a junior role. She has spotted the fact the company want an 'all-rounder', which can be code for 'entry-level role'. She also uses a touch of flattery and plenty of enthusiasm to gain attention.

Robert McLean
4/75 Allen Street
Hamilton QLD 4007

4 March 2013

Ms Priyanka Kapoor
HR Manager, Brown & Associates
Level 7 Central Plaza Two
66 Eagle Street
Brisbane QLD 4000

Dear Ms Kapoor

RE: Graduate Program Job No: AS782

I am applying for a highly sought after place in your next graduate intake as I am now in the final year of an Economics/Law degree (Honours) from the University of Queensland.

Please find enclosed a copy of my resume for your perusal. Of particular relevance is the summer clerkship I completed at Cooper Grace Ward in 2013 and the five-week work placement I completed at Leung, Chambers & Corr in Hong Kong in 2012.

I am interested in all facets of the law but have a strong interest in international business in particular. During my time in Hong Kong, I made several trips to China as an assistant to a team negotiating licensing agreements with manufacturers. I am also fluent in both written and spoken Mandarin and spoken Indonesian.

I would welcome an opportunity to speak with you in person about why I would make a good addition to the team at Brown & Associates.

Yours sincerely

Robert McLean

Figure 12-2: A sample cover letter from a graduate seeking work with an international law firm.

Lucy Roberts
27 Tranmere Street
Drummoyne NSW 2047

4 November 2013

Mr Mark Wilson
Creative Director, The Agency
82 Darling Street
Balmain NSW 2041

Dear Mr Wilson

RE: Content Producer Position (Ref. J784)

I am writing in response to your ad looking for a content producer and 'all-rounder' posted on Rachel's List.

Your agency has a reputation for excellence, collaboration and working with an impressive list of technology clients and I would love a chance to bring everything I've learnt and experienced to the team at The Agency.

Currently nearing the end of a postgraduate degree in creative intelligence and design, I have also been producing content and web-based advertising solutions during my holidays for such brands as Cat Cosmetics and ISC Software. In addition, my work history includes several customer-facing roles, making me well suited to the account service aspects of the role detailed in your ad.

Above all, I am a team player ready to jump in and assist no matter the task. I attach a copy of my resume and hope to get the opportunity to meet with you in person to discuss my application further.

Yours sincerely

Lucy Roberts

Figure 12-3: A sample cover letter from a postgraduate student applying for a role at a creative agency.

Tips for Grads Getting into the Game

Because school leavers and university graduates are new to the world of work and applying for jobs and graduate programs, making a few blunders isn't uncommon. Most new to the job game make mistakes simply through lack of experience. Here, we cover points to be mindful of when writing and sending your resume to help you avoid some common pitfalls:

✔ **Tell the truth, the whole truth:** Don't blow your job chances by fudging your university results, lying about past work experience or beefing up job titles. Be warned: Recruiters and employers are professional candidate screeners. They will check every claim you make.

✔ **Accentuate the positives:** A resume is a marketing document selling a product — you. Know your strong points and articulate these in your resume. If you're not sure what you're good at, ask someone who knows you well. Focus on your positives and don't draw attention to your negatives.

✔ **Be on time:** When applying for a specific job, traineeship, cadetship or graduate recruitment program, get your applications in by the due date or earlier. Many employers will not accept applications that arrive after the stated deadline.

✔ **Present well:** Make sure your resume is simple to read, easy to follow and free of spelling, grammatical and factual errors.

✔ **Don't be a copycat:** Never copy a friend's resume word-for-word (particularly if you're going for the same type of jobs). A recruiter receiving two identical resumes could dump both candidates. Graduate recruiters can also spot a copied template from a university careers website in an instant. Use the templates you find online as a guide only, and make sure you're creating a unique document. Everything on your resume must support your pitch for a job. Being a lazy copycat should not be part of your pitch — ever.

✔ **Get connected online:** Having social media skills is a plus in the digital age but only include a link to your blog, LinkedIn account or Instagram page in your resume if the content is strictly professional or academic. You can place the link below your contact details or add the detail to another section such as 'Extracurricular Activities' or 'Professional Development'. Also, search your own name online to see what is out there about you and change whatever you can if the information is unflattering or downright damaging.

We provide more information on social media and how it can support your resume in Chapter 8.

Great Websites for Graduates

Here are a few websites worth a look if you're hungry for graduate information, resume tips and career advice:

- ✔ **Graduate Careers Australia** (www.graduatecareers .com.au): A user-friendly, central source of information about graduate careers and employment, this site is jam-packed with articles to help you find a job.

- ✔ **Graduate Opportunities** (www.graduateopportunities .com): A great spot to search for vacation work, internships, graduate jobs, cadetships, scholarships, cooperatives and work experience programs. Provides statistical information on graduate employment, career advice, industry profiles and closing dates for applications.

- ✔ **JobSearch** (www.jobsearch.gov.au): Australia's largest employment portal, providing links to government graduate recruitment programs.

- ✔ **Unigrad** (www.unigrad.com.au): Fabulous careers and job search site for university students in Australia, including job listings, blogs, employer profiles and free job alerts.

- ✔ **GraduateJobs** (www.graduatejobs.com.au): Employment job board advertising graduate and entry-level jobs across Australia.

- ✔ **GradConnection** (au.gradconnection .com): Useful website connecting students with graduate opportunities. Research companies, get jobs delivered to your inbox and participate in forums.

- ✔ **NZ Uni Career Hub** (nzunicareerhub.ac.nz): Most of New Zealand's university career services use this site to post job vacancies directly from employers. Students can register for free to view jobs and info about graduate programs and employer-hosted events.

✔ **GradConnection NZ** (nz.gradconnection.com): This site offers job listings, advice, forums where you can ask questions and live chat sessions with employers.

Chapter 13

Applying for Government Positions

*A*pplying for a job in the public sector is a different kettle of fish to applying for a job in the private sector. Even if you have the most dazzling, eye-catching resume and have awesome experience, to score an interview for a government job you must follow the required process to the letter.

Although government departments do take into account your resume during the shortlisting process, your success depends more on how well you address the selection criteria, which we discuss in detail later in this chapter.

In this chapter, we talk about the government recruitment and selection process, public sector terms and where to go to get information about jobs. We describe what a typical written application includes and then advise what to keep in mind when you're writing or adapting your resume for a public service job. At the end of this chapter, we show you exactly how to address selection criteria using some helpful examples, and include tips for submitting your application. We have focused most of our attention in this chapter on addressing selection criteria for Australian-based jobs, because it can be a complex process.

Recruitment and Selection Process

When a permanent appointment needs to be filled in the public sector in Australia, a selection panel or committee is formed consisting of a chair and panel members. More often than not, a mix of genders and experience is included on the panel. The chair of the panel is usually the line manager or immediate supervisor of the work area, so knows the job role well. The other panel member(s) may be external or independent of the work area or a representative from the human resources department. The panel's first task is to read through and rate each written application on how well it meets the selection criteria. Applicants who score well in the written application generally land an interview.

In New Zealand, each sector advertises and appoints its own staff below the level of Chief Executive, and the process can differ from one organisation to another. Many agencies will require you to submit a resume and application form. Some, but not all, agencies require selection criteria to be addressed. In cases where selection criteria are used, you're expected to address these in the cover letter that accompanies your application.

Here's how a typical recruitment and selection process works in the public sector:

1. Vacancy or newly created position is flagged.

2. A position description (PD) is reviewed, developed or updated. If the PD is new or has changed significantly, it's evaluated to ascertain the work value of the job.

3. The position is advertised.

4. The selection panel is established. The panel consists of the chair and panel members.

5. The position closes. Applications are received and processed by the Human Resources (HR) department or shared service provider, and forwarded to the selection panel.

6. The panel agrees on the selection tools and benchmarks.

7. Applications are shortlisted according to benchmarks.

8. Shortlisted candidates are notified of an interview and in many cases the selection tools being used to assess their performance.

9. Shortlisted candidates are interviewed. Additional assessments may be conducted.

10. Referee checks are undertaken to verify suitability.

11. Panel reaches a selection decision.

12. Selection report is completed and approved by the delegate or relevant authority.

13. Successful candidate is made an offer of employment.

14. When the job offer is accepted, interviewed and unsuccessful applicants are advised of the selection outcome in Australia. In New Zealand, candidates shortlisted for interview and those who are unsuccessful are usually contacted at the same time. In many New Zealand agencies, internal candidates are declined verbally as well as in writing, while external candidates will be notified only in writing.

15. Post-selection feedback occurs.

Public Sector Terminology

Half the battle when you go for a government job is getting your head around all the public sector jargon. In Table 13-1, we point out some of the key terms used in the public sector and describe what they mean.

Table 13-1	Public Sector Terminology
Term	*Meaning*
Appoint	To employ a person in the public sector.
Ethical practice	Respecting the law and system of government, treating others fairly, being accountable for one's actions, displaying integrity and acting in the public interest. When you work in the public sector, the expectation is that you will behave and act ethically.
Equal Employment Opportunity (EEO)	EEO legislation prevents discrimination and harassment in the workplace. It's unlawful for any person to discriminate on the basis of age, sex, race, pregnancy, religion, disability, nationality, marital status, sexual preference or sexual identity, such as being transgender.

(continued)

Table 13-1 *(continued)*

Term	Meaning
Equity	Treating people fairly and with respect. All selection processes are required to be open, transparent, merit-based and free from discrimination and bias.
Merit	Selecting the best person for the job.
Selection criteria	Standards used to assess your skills, abilities, knowledge and qualifications.
Selection tools	Tools used to assess your performance against the selection criteria. Examples of selection tools include written application, resume, case studies, work test, assessment centres, interviews, computer test, presentation, role play, in-tray exercises, peer assessments, psychological tests, work samples and referee reports. For a range of agencies such as police and defence, physical assessments are also important selection tools.
Shortlist	The selection panel assesses each application according to how well it meets the selection criteria. Those that are successful make it onto a shortlist. Shortlisted applicants are assessed and compared against each other to find the best person for the job.
Workplace/ Occupational Health and Safety (WH&S)	WH&S legislation is designed to protect the health, safety and welfare of employees in the workplace. The Act imposes obligations on both employers and employees. Employers have a duty of care to inform, train and instruct employees in WH&S practices, check that all equipment, tools and machinery are safe, maintain safety records and ensure the safe use, storage and distribution of substances. Employees are required to follow WH&S instructions, use safety equipment supplied, attend training, notify managers of potential hazards, and work and behave in a manner that doesn't put others at risk.

Finding (And Researching) Government Jobs

Public sector jobs are often advertised in the following places:

- ✔ Local, national and regional newspapers.

- ✔ Online public sector job boards. For local government jobs, try careers.govt.nz in New Zealand and lgjobs.com.au in Australia. For federal jobs use jobs.govt.nz/ or jobsearch.gov.au or apsjobs.gov.au. States also have their own online job pages or websites:

  - jobs.nsw.gov.au

  - careers.nt.gov.au

  - qld.gov.au/jobs/

  - vacancies.sa.gov.au

  - jobs.tas.gov.au

  - careers.vic.gov.au

  - jobs.wa.gov.au

- ✔ Employment websites (for example, SEEK, CareerOne, MyCareer and the Australian Local Government Job Directory: job-directory.com.au in Australia; SEEK and TradeMe: trademe.co.nz/jobs in New Zealand).

- ✔ Websites of the various government departments; agencies and councils may also list their own jobs.

Before you even start writing your application, it's important to research the government agency and job to see if you have the skills, abilities, knowledge, qualifications and experience the panel is looking for. You can do this by

- ✔ **Downloading and reading through the position description carefully.** When a government vacancy is advertised in Australia and New Zealand, it's usually accompanied by a position description that describes the nitty-gritty on both the organisation and job. The position description includes the job's title, classification/level, division/branch/work unit, location, salary level or grade, job/vacancy reference number, purpose, environment, reporting relationships and duty statement/role description. The closing date for applications and the name and phone number of a contact officer you can call for more information is usually in the job ad.

The position description is extremely important because it contains the selection criteria that you need to address in your written application. You can obtain a copy of the position description by

- Ringing the contact person or the department's enquiry number listed in the job ad and asking for a position description to be posted, faxed or emailed to you.

- Downloading a copy from the public sector job board or employment website where the position was advertised.

- Printing the position description from the council or agency website.

✓ **Making use of additional info on the public sector job board.** Some government agencies provide additional information to assist you complete your application. You can get hold of the material by downloading the relevant attachments from the public sector job board, employment website or agency's site. Additional documents can include all or some of the following: Application cover sheet, position description, applicant information package/ kit, application guidelines and employment declarations. *Note:* The application guide or information package/kit is very handy because it can give you an overview of the organisation and how to apply for jobs.

✓ **Speaking to the contact officer.** If you have specific questions about the job or work area, talk to the contact person on the telephone number listed in the advertisement, on the public sector job board or in the position description. This person knows the job back to front and is usually the chair of the panel or manager of the work area. It's always a good idea to ask why the position is vacant and see if anyone is acting or working temporarily in the role.

✓ **Exploring the agency's website.** Go to the agency's website to learn more about the organisation and what it does. Include in your application any relevant information you find here — you'll immediately stand out from the pack and the panel will be impressed by your initiative.

✓ **Accessing other information.** Get your hands on any available literature, such as annual reports, business and corporate plans, media releases, information sheets, newsletters and brochures.

Compiling Your Written Application

Most public sector jobs require you to pull together a written application, which usually consists of the following:

- ✓ **Application cover sheet.** If you want to go for a government job, you need to fill in and attach a cover sheet to the front of your application. Each agency has its own. You can get a copy of the form by downloading it from the public sector job board or government agency website. If you're applying online, the cover sheet may be incorporated in the online application form.

- ✓ **Cover letter (sometimes optional).** Tell the panel a little more about yourself using a well-designed cover letter.

- ✓ **Resume with names of two or three referees.** Create an eye-catching, professional resume tailored to the position and emphasise any previous experience that relates to the job. Refer to Chapter 3 for more detail. Include the names, positions and contact details for two work-related referees (preferably your current or previous supervisors). Remember to get the okay first, before nominating referees. For more information, see the following section.

- ✓ **Responses to the selection criteria/statement of claims.** This is the most important part of your application. You need to respond to all the selection criteria or key capabilities contained within the position description. Depending on the government agency, you may be asked to address each criterion as a separate heading, outlining your knowledge, understanding or experience in an area. Alternatively you may be asked to write a written statement or incorporate your selection criteria into your cover letter outlining your suitability for the role. We show you how, in 'Sorting Out Selection Criteria' later in this chapter.

Update your referees

If you're going for a government job, a good idea is to send your referees a copy of the job's position description and selection criteria. They may need to answer questions about you in relation to the selection criteria down the track. We provide more information on managing referees in Chapter 3.

Preparing a Government Resume

While a resume for the public service is much the same as a private sector resume, you do want to keep a few extra things in mind if you're putting together a public sector resume for the first time:

- ✔ **Provide enough information.** One-page resumes can't tell the panel much; aim for three to four pages.

- ✔ **Avoid acronyms.** Don't assume everyone reading your resume will know the ins and outs of what you do or the previous positions you've held. Spell out in full any fancy terms, department- or organisation-specific acronyms, and explain your past roles simply and accurately.

- ✔ **Give fancy folders and coloured paper the flick.** If you're sending a hard-copy application, keep it simple and straightforward — black ink on white paper, stapled in the top left corner.

- ✔ **Include referees in your resume.** When applying for government positions, always include the details of your referees in your resume. Writing 'Referees available upon request' won't wash.

Sorting Out Selection Criteria

Selection criteria information appears in the position description, and is the government's way of finding the right person for the job. You need to address the selection criteria effectively to progress to the next stage of the process. You'll often see selection criteria written as statements or as key capabilities and competencies.

Demonstrating that you meet the required selection criteria is not a step in the application process you can skip or rush, so make sure you check the deadline for applications first and leave plenty of time in which to prepare your application.

Here's an example selection criteria statement:

1. Well-developed written and oral communication skills with a proven ability to negotiate with external clients.

The following examples show different ways capability-based selection criteria may be presented.

Example 1:

Communicates with Influence

- Demonstrates an ability to communicate, both verbally and in writing, with a wide range of stakeholders in an accurate, timely and unambiguous manner.

Example 2:

Cultivate Strong Working Relationships

- Establish professional relationships with a range of internal and external clients and stakeholders.
- Work collaboratively as a team member and provide effective support to other team members.
- Acknowledge the achievements of other staff.
- Support and respect individual and organisational differences and diversity.
- Provide guidance and direction to more junior or inexperienced staff.

Example 3:

Innovates

- Provide an example that demonstrates your ability to respond flexibly to changing demands in the workplace.
- Describe a time you contributed ideas to improve efficiency in the workplace.

Selection criteria can be classified as essential or desirable:

- ✔ **Essential:** No buts about it, you must be able to meet these selection criteria in order to apply for the job.
- ✔ **Desirable:** If you have these skills, qualifications or knowledge, you're in front. If you can, try to address these criteria.

Presenting selection criteria

Handwritten applications are rare these days but if you're tempted — resist. Always type your application using a standard typeface such as Arial or Times New Roman, in 11- or 12-point (size). Stick to a single typeface for the main text and use bold for headings or emphasis.

The government department folk like you to present your resume and selection criteria as two separate documents. Mixing them together gets confusing. Put a cover page on your selection criteria that includes the name of the position, the vacancy/job reference number, your contact details and the title of the document, as shown in Figure 13-1.

STATEMENT ADDRESSING THE SELECTION CRITERIA

CUSTOMER SERVICE OFFICER (Grade 3)
JOB REF: 35/01/9070/4

Name: Lisa Moore
Address: 33 Silkwood Road,
               Shorncliffe Qld 4017
Telephone: (07) 1111 1111
Email: lmoore@email.com.au

Figure 13-1: Sample cover page — for selection criteria.

Using the correct format

When completing an Australian government online application, you may be asked to place your responses to questions under particular headings. This could happen in two ways. You could be asked to type or cut-and-paste your selection criteria responses into the text fields provided on an application document. However, where that is not the case and you're required to attach your selection criteria document using particular headings to separate out your response to each criterion, we suggest using the following logical and easy-to-read format:

- ✔ **Order your criteria.** List your criteria in numbered order — for example, SC1 (for the first selection criterion), then SC2 and so on. Bold each criterion heading to make it stand out.

- ✔ **Use headers and footers.** Put your name, the position title and vacancy/job reference number either in the header or footer. Number each page.

✔ **Use white space.** Avoid smothering the reader with too much text. Remember to use plenty of open white space. Use single-line spacing and standard default margins.

✔ **Make 'I' statements.** For example, 'In my role as Administration Officer, I was responsible for . . .'.

✔ **Avoid using passive language.** For example, 'I prepared detailed reports' sounds more powerful than 'Detailed reports were prepared by me'.

✔ **Stick to word counts.** Keep to agency word limits. Some departments won't accept text over the stated word limit. If no word limit is given, try to write no more than a couple of paragraphs per selection criteria. Aim to address all the criteria in two to three pages max. If in doubt, check with the contact officer as to the agency's preference.

In New Zealand, not all agencies use selection criteria. Those that do expect the selection criteria to be addressed in the application form or cover letter, over about a page.

Many New Zealand government jobs will include a link to a detailed position description (PD). We recommend you access the position description and use it to tailor your application for New Zealand government roles. The PD is packed with useful information — who the role reports to and interacts with, the purpose of the role, the key accountabilities for the role and the personal and professional attributes you need to have to land the job.

Deciphering selection criteria

In this section we outline the different components used in selection criteria in Australia, and how to discern the requirements.

Selection criteria statements

You can get a grip on all that government gobbledegook if you break down the selection criteria statements into manageable steps, as follows:

1. **Read through the selection criteria carefully and underline the key phrases.**

   Key phrases tell you what the criteria is asking you to do: Are you required to give an example to display your experience? Does the reader want you to demonstrate your knowledge? Or do you need to show you understand the concepts? Key phrases are often the first one or two words of the statement; however, they can be scattered throughout the selection criteria. Table 13-2 provides a list of common key phrases used in the public sector.

Table 13-2	Key Phrases for Selection Criteria
Key Phrase	*What Your Response Should Address*
Ability to	You may not have performed the specific task before, but you show that you have potential to acquire the relevant skills, abilities and knowledge. Use examples that highlight your transferable skills.
Awareness	You're somewhat familiar with the content.
Capacity	You have the necessary skills, but you may not have applied them in a work context.
Demonstrated	You're required to give a specific example from your work experience.
Experience	You have performed the duties in the past. Outline the extent of your experience and describe what was required in the job.
High level, well developed, superior, outstanding, strong	You must prove you have advanced skills, knowledge and abilities. Use a real-life example highlighting your achievements in the area.
Knowledge	You must show the reader you're familiar with the subject matter. Explain how you acquired or applied the knowledge gained through your work experience or learnings.
Mandatory, possession	This is an absolute requirement of the position — for example, a university degree or equivalent, driver's licence or a professional registration.
Proven	You have successfully performed the activity in the past and can back up your claims with supporting evidence.
Understanding	You don't just have knowledge of the topic, you comprehend the material and grasp its significance.

2. **Note the keywords that identify required knowledge, skills and personal attributes.**

   Keywords are the topics you address in your written application. You need to spot all the keywords to address the selection criteria fully. A good technique to identify the keywords that you need to use is to underline the key phrases in the position description. Use these as pointers to the knowledge, skills and personal attributes the position is looking for. For example, suppose you have underlined the key phrases (refer to Table 13-2) in the following:

   > SC1 <u>**Demonstrated**</u> **customer service skills** with a <u>**proven ability**</u> to work both **autonomously** and in a **team environment.**

   Now go to the key phrase 'demonstrated' and ask yourself, 'What do they want me to demonstrate?' You can see then that 'customer service skills' is a keyword. Likewise, look at 'proven ability' and say to yourself 'What do they want me to prove?' You can identify 'autonomously' and 'team environment' as two other keywords.

3. **Write your response showing how your qualifications meet the criterion.**

   So, to address the criteria in Step 2, you need to give a specific example of a time when you displayed customer service skills, a specific example of a time when you worked autonomously, and a specific example of a time when you contributed to a team environment.

   See the next section on writing responses to selection criteria.

Capability-based selection criteria

For capability-based selection criteria, the process is a little different. The capability is often stated upfront with a list of descriptors underneath. Here's an example to illustrate:

Exemplify Personal Drive and Integrity **(Capability)**

(Descriptors)

- ✔ Demonstrate a high level of professionalism, independence, integrity and accountability
- ✔ Have a positive work orientation

- ✔ Promote and uphold APS values, APS Code of Conduct, Agency's Code of Conduct and other ethical and professional standards

- ✔ Exhibit initiative, motivation and energy

- ✔ Display resilience, commitment, courage and tact

- ✔ Value learning and commit to continuing professional development

With capabilities, you don't need to address each bullet point as a separate selection criterion. The descriptors underneath each capability heading outline what's expected at a particular classification level. They tell you what the capability means. Descriptors are guidelines only. You need to give an example of a specific situation where you have demonstrated the capability, taking into consideration the descriptors when framing your response. Be sure to include recent examples.

Most agencies will have their own guidelines for addressing capability-based selection criteria. Your best bet is to check out the agency's website or government job board to see if additional information is available on how to address the key capabilities.

You can find information about how to address selection criteria in the Australian Public Service by downloading the document *Cracking the Code* available from the Australian Public Service Commission website: Visit www.apsc.gov.au.

Writing responses to selection criteria

You know what you need to write about; the next step is getting it down. In this section, we talk about how to structure your response to the selection criteria. We also show you examples of written responses.

Structuring your response

Use this framework as a guide to help put together your own selection criteria responses:

1. **Note the selection criteria.**

   List the selection criteria at the top of the page.

2. **Start with an initial statement.**

   Begin with an initial statement that tells the reader you meet the selection criteria. Here are a few examples:

SC1 High-level written communication skills

I possess a high level of written communication skills ...

SC2 Demonstrated customer service skills

With over five years' experience as a Customer Service Representative in a call centre, I have developed outstanding customer service skills ...

SC3 Well-developed supervisory skills

Throughout the last five years, particularly in my role as Team Leader, I have developed strong supervisory skills ...

SC4 Excellent organisational skills with a proven ability to coordinate events

As an Administrative Assistant at ABC Company, I was responsible for coordinating a number of events that required excellent organisational skills ...

SC5 Demonstrated understanding of Equal Employment Opportunity

I have a very good understanding of Equal Employment Opportunity legislation, having worked as an Industrial Relations Consultant for over seven years ...

SC6 Ability to work effectively in a team environment

My role as University Fundraising Coordinator involved working effectively in a team ...

3. **Provide a supporting statement.**

Now, expand on your initial statement by showing *how* you meet the criterion. Walk the reader through an example that clearly demonstrates how you put the skills or knowledge into practice. One method you can use to construct your examples is the STAR method, invented by Development Dimensions International, Inc (DDI).

STAR stands for:

- ✔ **Situation/Task.** Explain the circumstances. The Situation or Task is the background or context in which you took action. It explains why you acted in a particular manner.

- ✔ **Action.** Describe what you did. An Action is what you said or did in response to a Situation or Task.

> ✔ **Result.** Describe the outcome of the actions. A Result is the effect of your Actions. They tell recruiters what changes or differences the person's actions made and whether the actions were effective and appropriate.

© Development Dimensions International (DDI). Reproduced with permission.

Examples of selection criteria

Here are sample responses to two selection criteria that require applicants to have *knowledge* and *understanding* of Workplace Health and Safety (WHS) legislation and requirements.

Showing good working knowledge

Here's an example displaying good working knowledge.

SC1 Knowledge of Workplace Health and Safety

I have developed a good working knowledge of Workplace Health and Safety (WH&S) gained throughout my career in the public sector. As a HR Consultant at ABC Department, I attended induction training that provided information on the Act, location of fire exits, emergency equipment, first aid facilities, workplace health and safety officers and evacuation assembly points. I have also read workplace health and safety pamphlets and have familiarised myself with safety policies, procedures and guidelines on the department's intranet. Recently, I participated in a half-day workplace health and safety workshop, which covered ergonomics and safe lifting procedures. In addition to this, I majored in Human Resource Management at university and achieved a high distinction grade for the subject Health and Safety in the Workplace.

I am aware that the main objective of the [name of the Act] is to prevent the occurrence of death, injury and illness in the workplace. The [name of the Act] is a framework that places obligations on both employers and employees to minimise exposure to risk. As an employee, I have a duty of care to comply with workplace health and safety requirements, participate in training, report potential hazards to my supervisor, use protective equipment supplied, not interfere or misuse equipment or wilfully endanger the health and safety of any other person.

When the selection criterion requires *knowledge* you need to show the panel that you're familiar with the material and know the fundamentals of any relevant legislation. Always mention how you acquired the knowledge. If you can, go the extra mile by giving an example that clearly demonstrates how you applied the knowledge in the past.

Displaying deeper understanding

Here's an example showing deeper understanding of the legislation.

> **SC2 Understanding of Workplace Health and Safety**
>
> With over seven years' experience as a Call Centre Team Leader, I have developed an excellent understanding of workplace health and safety. As a manager at XYZ Bank, I'm aware of my responsibilities under the [name of the Act] to protect the health, safety and wellbeing of all my employees.
>
> Managing risk inside the call centre has involved ensuring walkways, entrances and emergency exits are free of obstructions to avoid accidents and injuries. I also encourage staff to adopt safe work practices by adjusting headsets, chairs and screens regularly to reduce the risk of muscular injuries. I monitor the temperature inside the call centre and ensure staff drink plenty of water and take regular stretch and rest breaks. New staff are inducted into call centre health and safety. I perform regular audits and conduct in-house WHS training. All staff are advised of reporting procedures for identifying hazards and the correct process to follow in the event of acoustic shock. Adopting safe work practices in the call centre has resulted in decreased absenteeism and turnover, reduced workplace stress, higher morale and lower costs associated with work-related accidents and injuries.

When the selection criterion requires an *understanding*, you need to go further than just knowing what it is. You need to be able to show you comprehend the material and understand its significance in the workplace.

Demonstrating your experience

When you're required to *demonstrate* or *prove* that you have experience in a certain area, putting ideas into words can sometimes be difficult. Here are some nifty ideas to help you answer these kinds of selection criteria:

- ✓ Be specific.

- ✓ Use an example from your work experience that demonstrates your skills, abilities and knowledge.

- ✓ Provide evidence of how you applied the capability. Describe in your example the process or actions undertaken to address the situation.

- ✓ Focus on the outcome achieved.

- ✓ Use the STAR method mentioned earlier in this chapter as a framework to structure your response.

Begin by brainstorming — think about what you did on a daily basis. We provide an example using the STAR method here:

SC3 Demonstrated Ability to Maintain a Safe Work Environment

Situation:

Throughout the last five years, particularly in my role as Workplace Health and Safety Officer at ABC Trades College, I have demonstrated my ability to maintain a safe work environment.

Task:

In this position, I investigate incidents and recommend changes to improve the health and safety of the workplace. Recently, a second-year apprentice glazier severed his thumb pressing glass into a window frame. Pressure was applied to the middle of the glass instead of the outer edges, which caused the glass to shatter and resulted in his injury.

Action:

Once the incident had been reported I asked the teacher to complete an Incident Notification Form and conducted a risk assessment of the work area to review the cause and circumstance surrounding the incident.

Factors included no personal protective equipment (PPE) on the hands of the apprentice at the time of the event, and the apprentice's inability to follow work procedures and instructions properly. Based on the investigation, I prepared a Workplace Health and Safety Assessment report for the Program Manager and recommended that apprentice glaziers wear protective gloves and wrist guards during practical classes to avoid injury. The injured apprentice was to receive appropriate training and instruction in correct glazing procedures, and existing procedures were to be amended to incorporate the use of PPE. All apprentice glaziers were encouraged to undergo refresher induction training on the safe handling of glass and ongoing reviews of the window framing module were to be made.

Result:

All of the recommendations were endorsed by senior management. Workplace Health and Safety reports for the July quarter have revealed a 75% reduction in glass and glazing lacerations since implementation of the new procedure.

Note: Don't use the STAR headings included in this example when writing your own responses: These are included as a guide here.

When it comes to writing your responses to the selection criteria, don't leave it till the last minute. Putting together a quality application takes time.

Always read through the duty or role statement in the position description before writing your selection criteria responses. In your written application, include examples that show the panel that you've performed the duties or similar duties in the past.

If you're an internal candidate, make sure you don't leave out important information in your application. Even if you know the panel members, never assume they have prior knowledge of you or your work.

Sending Off Your Government Application

Here are a few handy hints for you to consider before shooting off your application for a government job, depending on which delivery method you're planning to use:

✔ **Hand delivering or posting by mail.** If you're sending your written application by post or delivering your application in person, check the job application to see if more than one copy of the documentation is required. Some government departments in Australia ask for an original plus two copies of your written application — one for each of the panel members. However, you only need to send one copy of the application cover sheet. If you're applying for more than one government job, remember to complete a separate application for each job/vacancy reference number.

When sending a paper-based application by mail, staple all parts of the application together.

If you're submitting your application by post, always factor in time for unexpected delays. For example, if you normally allow one day for mail delivery, allow several days, just to be on the safe side.

✔ **Faxing.** If you're faxing your application, feed the originals through the fax machine. Do not use coloured paper.

✔ **Sending by email.** If the department requires you to email your application, put all the documents in one email attachment that contains the cover letter, resume and selection criteria. In some cases, you may need to attach the cover sheet separately. Include the job/vacancy reference number in the subject line of the email. Send your file attachment in a standard document that the recruiter will be able to open (check format requirements first if you're not sure).

Avoid emailing (or faxing) your application during peak times when you may experience transmission delays. Be organised and get your application in early!

✔ **Applying online.** Most government departments prefer you to submit online applications. If you're submitting an online application through a government website, follow the instructions carefully and attach all documents in the required file format. Don't skip any of the selection criteria either — you want to maximise your chances of getting an interview.

Always keep to file size or word limits if you're sending an online application. Some systems will automatically cut off responses that exceed the specified word limit.

If you are applying online, don't double up by posting, faxing or emailing additional copies of your application. One copy is enough.

Avoid uploading zipped files, protected documents or tagged PDFs that may be difficult for recruiters to open.

Don't blow your job chances by submitting a late application. It's your responsibility to get your application in before the stated closing date and time. Some agencies will acknowledge receipt of your application by email, post or online.

After you submit your application, allow at least a couple of weeks for the panel to sift through the pile of applications. If it's been awhile and you haven't heard back, ring the contact officer listed in the advertisement for more information. If you're shortlisted, the panel will be in touch with you to arrange an interview. If you're not shortlisted, you'll be notified of the outcome in writing.

If you were unsuccessful, you can contact the chair of the selection panel when the process has been finalised and ask for feedback. Post-selection feedback is often available upon request. This is not always the case, however. For example, a New Zealand government recruiter told us about a campaign that attracted 30,000 applications for 7,500 jobs. In such cases, providing feedback to every candidate was impossible. Feedback will be based on your performance in relation to the selection criteria.

Part V

The Part of Tens

the part of tens

In this part...

- ✔ Discover the resume wrongs that really irritate recruitment consultants — lengthy resumes, spelling mistakes, employment dates not listed in months and years; the list goes on and on.

- ✔ Explore simple ways you can present and lay out your resume so that it looks attractive and inviting to read.

Chapter 14

Ten Sure-Fire Ways to Turn Off a Recruitment Consultant

• •

In This Chapter

▶ Discovering the pet hates of recruitment consultants

▶ Revealing insider hints and tips

▶ Submitting resumes to recruitment agencies

• •

*R*ecruitment agencies are the gatekeepers to a huge number of permanent, temporary or contract jobs in Australia and New Zealand. If you don't impress the recruiter, your resume will never be seen by the right employer. Recruitment consultants are the experts when it comes to recruitment, and get their thrills from finding you work, filling jobs and putting your resume forward for jobs. But have you ever wondered what recruitment agencies really think about the resumes they receive? Want to know what cheeses off recruiters and what gets their blood boiling?

Read this chapter to find out the specific details of resume wrongs. We've surveyed loads of recruitment consultants to identify their ten biggest resume turn-offs — the things that irk them, tick them right off or drive them up the wall (you get the message) so you can avoid these pitfalls.

Up Close and Too Personal

One sure-fire way to turn off a recruitment consultant is by providing too much information in your resume. The fact that you're a fitness fanatic with two dogs, three cats, a Mexican walking fish and a husband who's president of the local football club is nobody's business but your own, and you shouldn't bombard recruiters with this kind of detail. Keep your resume simple. Remember to market your skills and abilities to a recruitment consultant by only focusing on the areas that count.

Never disclose personal details in your resume, such as your date of birth, religion, sex or marital status, or the names and ages of your children. This information is irrelevant to getting a job, so omit them from your resume altogether. (Refer to Chapter 3 for more on what to include, and what not to include, in your resume.)

Date Hate

Here are recruitment consultants' pet peeves when it comes to dates shown in resumes:

- ✔ Omitting start or end dates for jobs

- ✔ Listing years only (for example, '2012 – 2013' — was it one month or twelve?)

- ✔ Falsifying or fudging employment dates. (Dates of employment are validated in the referee checks, so be careful not to do this.)

- ✔ Substituting years for exact dates, especially in your most recent jobs (for example, 'Three years at Fergusson and Taylor Accountants' rather than 'Fergusson and Taylor Accountants, July 2011 – May 2014')

Nothing beats a resume that's sequential and easy to follow. Win over a recruitment consultant by listing months and years of employment for each job in your work history, as shown here:

July 2012 – August 2013   **Teacher's Aide**

St Stephen's Primary School

Begin your work history by listing your most recent job first, going backwards. If you have any glaring gaps that stand out like a pirate's missing teeth, be honest and fill the gaps with explanations of what's been going on. Recruitment consultants recognise the fact that people take time off to study, raise a family and travel. Refer to Chapter 2 for more on resume formats and Chapter 5 for tips on managing gaps in your resume.

Peeved Off with Resume Length

Resumes that are too long or too short really annoy recruitment consultants. The tricky thing about the acceptable length of a resume is that it can vary. As a safe bet, stick to around two to three pages if you're early in your career and up to four pages if you're more established. In talking to recruitment consultants, we've heard that keeping a resume to just a few pages is appreciated. If you're not sure about length, why not ask the recruitment agency you're registered with for advice?

Here are a few points to consider when preparing your resume from scratch:

- ✔ Having to slog through resumes written in essay or letter style is about as torturous as reading the dictionary from cover to cover. Recruitment consultants love white space and plenty of bullet points.

- ✔ Reading a one-page resume can be likened to going to a restaurant and only receiving half the food you ordered. You crave for more. Don't skimp on the content. Resumes with substance win hands down.

- ✔ Wading through a truckload of waffle is as appealing as sitting in a crowded bus on a hot summer's day. Focus on quality rather than quantity. Recruiters want to read two pages of quality material, not 20 pages of irrelevant detail. Avoid bulking up your resume with useless information, such as swimming awards going back to Year 4 or high school certificates dating back to the 1970s. Think of your resume as valuable real estate: Don't squander a single centimetre with unnecessary information.

Who Dunnit?

Missing contact details and incomplete information scores very low on a recruiter's scale of first impressions. Recruitment consultants don't have time for detective work. For example, if you offer no clues on your whereabouts, you may miss out on potential job opportunities. It sounds obvious, but make sure your contact details are correct and current.

Recruiters want to see your

- ✔ Telephone numbers — mobile, work and home.
- ✔ Email addresses — both work and home.
- ✔ Home or postal address, including suburb, state and city.

Always put your contact details on every page of your resume in case a recruitment consultant prints it out and the pages get separated.

Never list your contact details in a tiny font in the document's header or footer. This important information needs to be visible and easy to read.

Being Contactable

Mobile phones can be a sore point for recruiters, especially when the recruiter is unable to contact you or leave a message. Keep in mind the following when applying for jobs through an agency:

- ✔ Don't let your mobile phone ring out when a potential job is in the pipeline. Nothing frustrates a recruiter more than this. If your line is busy, you can't take the call, your phone is out of range or your battery is flat, divert your mobile to voicemail so the recruiter can leave a message.
- ✔ Record a professional voicemail greeting.
- ✔ Recharge your mobile phone and check your messages regularly.
- ✔ Don't let your phone become inactive (for example, if you're on a pre-paid mobile plan). Always top up the credit, so you can retrieve your voicemail messages.

Ticked Off About Referees

When it comes to referees, here are a few things that can tick off a recruitment consultant:

- ✔ **Failing to list referees.** Make sure you mention referees in your resume. Either jot down referee details (as we mention in Chapter 3) or write 'Referees available upon request'. If you use the term 'Referees available upon request' in your resume, always remember to bring your referee details to the interview — and to have the details ready and waiting for that request!

- ✔ **Including referees who have moved on.** Keep in contact with your referees and track down the relevant details if they switched jobs. Also, it's important to keep them in the loop with regards to your job movements. Remember, it's your responsibility to chase this up, not the recruitment consultant's.

- ✔ **Going overboard with written references.** Although you may be proud of your written references, the grim truth is they aren't given much credibility these days, and recruitment consultants rarely read them. If you want to impress a recruitment consultant, highlight two or three work-related referees in your resume.

- ✔ **Using referees way past their expiry date.** Whatever you do, don't list referees that go way back. Most recruitment consultants want up-to-date referees who can comment on your work performance over the past couple of years. Often, referees who worked with you eons ago struggle to recall how punctual you were, the quality of your work and so on.

Achieving Nothing

So you think you're the best candidate for the job . . . Well, it's time for you to get out there and market yourself with a standout resume. Don't be shy when it comes to your resume. A recruiter finds nothing as annoying as a resume that doesn't list awards and achievements. Remember, a recruitment consultant has to sell you to his or her clients — in other words, your potential employers. By not quantifying your achievements, nor listing your strengths in your resume, you run the risk of being glossed over.

Liven up your resume with quantifiable achievements. Dazzle the recruiter with results and showcase the fact you saved your past employer millions, reduced turnover, increased sales, generated profits or initiated something new. Believe it or not, achievements grab attention and inspire confidence in your abilities. Recruitment consultants love 'em! We show you how to construct achievements in Chapter 3.

Lack of Detail

Recruitment consultants are clever but they don't know everything. Receiving resumes with limited explanation about what companies do and specialise in can be frustrating.

If you have been working internationally or in small offices, chances are most recruitment consultants won't know the companies listed in your work history, or have a clue about what they do. A great way to shed some light on a past place of employment is to include a brief statement or explanatory paragraph, detailing the following:

- ✔ The type of industry the company operates in

- ✔ What the business or organisation specialises in

- ✔ The number of staff in the organisation

- ✔ The annual turnover of the company

- ✔ Who you reported to and what your role was

Looking at the following examples, chances are most employers won't know or have even heard of 'Deluxe Home Goods' or 'Protect Us'. Including an introductory spiel at the beginning of your work history helps to create some meaningful context straightaway. This is much better than saying nothing. As you can see, the recruiter gets a clear idea of the company background, its size, what products and services it specialises in and its annual turnover. Notice how the 'Deluxe Home Goods' example goes that little bit further by listing a company description, followed by a brief statement identifying the manager's accountabilities and who the person reported to.

Reception/Administration Officer

Protect Us

About the company: Protect Us is a small Australian security firm, specialising in the provision of monitored intruder alarms, surveillance cameras and access control systems. The company employs three staff with a turnover in excess of $1M.

Financial Controller

Deluxe Home Goods

About Deluxe Home Goods: Headquartered in New Zealand, the company designs, manufactures and markets household appliances to the global market. Deluxe has manufacturing plants in South America, China and Australia and has a total turnover in excess of NZ$1.2 billion. The company directly employs 300 people in Australia. Reporting to the Group Managing Director, Australia, I held the position of Financial Controller, Manufacturing Division and directly supervised a finance team of 10.

Sending Spam

Spamming resumes here, there and everywhere, and applying for every job under the sun regardless of whether or not the position really interests you, is likely to brand you as a 'tyre-kicker', 'professional job hunter' or a 'specialist of nothing'.

One big turn-off for recruitment consultants are resumes that are too general and not tailored to specific jobs. When it comes to jobs, don't take the lazy option of using a generic one-size-fits-all resume. Trim and tailor your resume to the job. You can do this by

✔ Scanning the job ad and incorporating the skills you have with the skills required in a summary of yourself at the beginning of your resume.

✔ Emphasising and de-emphasising jobs. Display job duties and achievements for job positions you want to highlight and promote and leave out details of jobs that aren't relevant.

✔ Adding value to your resume by including professional development courses, memberships, IT skills or anything that relates to the job and portrays you in a positive light.

In Chapter 3 we provide more details on how to tailor your resume for a particular role.

General Stuff You Don't Want to Get Wrong

Here are seven no-no's that drive recruitment consultants crazy when reading through piles of job application letters and resumes:

- ✔ **Being inconsistent.** Don't say in your resume that you want to pursue a career with a large multinational company and then apply for a position in a small firm. Be consistent and know what you want.

- ✔ **Making spelling errors and typos.** Addressing a covering letter to Mrs Hill-Murphy instead of Mrs Johnstone from Hill and Murphy is simply not on.

- ✔ **Submitting applications for the wrong job.** What do you think this says about your attention to detail?

- ✔ **Forgetting to attach your resume.** A simple mistake like this may cost you a job. Always check your resume is attached before you hit the send button.

- ✔ **Applying for jobs that are out of your reach.** Just as it's silly to wear a fleecy tracksuit on the beach in summer, applying for jobs when you're clearly unqualified is both a waste of your time and a consultant's. Why apply for a pilot's role if you can't fly a plane?

- ✔ **Using general rather than specific terms.** Saying you worked for a financial services organisation is no substitute for saying you worked for Bourke and Wills Bank. Recruitment consultants want specifics.

- ✔ **Being creative with the truth.** Remember how we referred to recruitment consultants as 'experts' at the beginning of this chapter? Well, most can smell a fib or an exaggeration a kilometre away. Stretching the truth and beefing up your resume using fluffy titles for past jobs does nothing to impress a recruitment consultant. Don't pretend to be something you're not, and never lie about past employment. It will all come out in the wash when your claims are validated, or refuted, by referees.

Chapter 15

Ten Tips for Perfect Presentation

*S*o, your resume seduces recruiters with its wonderful content, but seems to be lacking in the presentation department. Maybe you need a little guidance on how to give your formatted resume a smart and professional look? Here are ten presentation tips to help transform even the plainest resume into a sizzling, eye-catching sensation.

Working Out Word Processing

Create your winning resume using a standard word-processing program like Microsoft Word. The beauty of Word is that most recruiters have access to the software, so opening attachments is easy.

Before you send your resume to a recruitment agency or employer, check to see you're submitting it in the preferred format. Even better, ring the agency and find out. Microsoft Word is pretty much the agency favourite these days rather than a PDF document because it allows for easy editing. While your resume may be perfection itself, recruitment agencies may need to make some changes to suit their processes. These include removing your name and contact details before your resume is sent to a client, and also being able to cut and paste your resume into their own agency template.

Recruiters still want to receive your resume in a conventional format (for more on this, refer to Chapter 2), but once they have it, they want the freedom to work with the content in a way that meets their needs.

 Don't submit a handwritten resume — you run the risk of being perceived as a 'technophobic fuddy-duddy'. Keep up with the times and use a computer. If you don't own a computer, here are some easy ways to access one:

- ✔ Type your resume on a friend's computer
- ✔ Reserve a PC at your local council library or visit an internet cafe
- ✔ Rent a computer
- ✔ Access a computer at your school, university or college

Computer skills are pretty much a must these days so if you need to boost your IT skills, consider some training, such as enrolling in a class at TAFE or a community college.

Using Standard Fonts

Fancy fonts don't cut it when it comes to resumes. Stick to using common fonts (also called typefaces) such as Times New Roman, Arial, Garamond, Verdana, Tahoma, Calibri and Century Schoolbook. These styles are simple, easy to read and scream professionalism. As a general rule, choose 11 or 12 point (size of the letters) for the main text, and 12 or 14 point for section headings. These are summarised in Table 15-1.

Table 15-1	Fonts and Point Sizes	
Font	*Main Text*	*Section Heading*
Arial	11	12 or 14
Calibri	11	12
Century Schoolbook	11	12
Garamond	12	14
Tahoma	10	12
Times New Roman	11 or 12	12 or 14
Verdana	10	12

Use fonts carefully and cleverly. However, don't go overboard:

- ✔ **Don't be tempted to use elaborate fonts.** Flowery or swirling fonts, while attractive, create hassles for recruiters because they're difficult to read both on and off the screen.

- ✔ **Don't clutter your resume by using too many fonts.** Choose one or two fonts and use these tastefully throughout your resume.

- ✔ **Don't overdo it with bold and CAPITALS.** Also avoid italics or underlining if your document is to be read by scanners.

- ✔ **Don't use small fonts.** This is annoying for recruiters — too hard on the eyes. Refer to Table 15-1 for recommended fonts and point sizes.

- ✔ **Don't use colours.** Black and white works best unless you're applying for a design position.

Choosing Plain Paper

Since most resumes are sent to employers via email, don't squander your money on expensive paper — even if sending a hard copy. How your resume feels in your hands won't get you the job; the quality of the content will.

If you do print your resume on paper that has more weight and texture than photocopying paper, use conservative colours such as white or off-white, which is easy to photocopy or fax. Also, stay away from glossy, marbled, speckled, patterned or textured paper. A recruiter will need to scan your resume into his or her database and this paper does not scan well.

Getting the Right Look

Keep your resume simple and easy to read. Be consistent with your formatting, writing style and spacing. For example, if you bullet point your responsibilities and achievements for one job, do the same for your previous positions. If you bold one job title in your work history, make sure you highlight the rest. Consider these points:

- ✔ Keep font type and point sizes the same for section headings, subheadings and main text. Left align or centre your headings.

✔ Check for uniformity when listing dates. Format dates of employment in months and years or years only, but never combine both. Stick to using one one date style (for example, November 2013 or 01/14) throughout your resume. Put all dates on the one side of the page.

✔ Ensure section headings, sub-headings and job titles stand out.

✔ Make sure all text, bullet points and headings line up perfectly. Left align or justify the main text.

✔ Don't overkill with bullet points. Use one or two different styles of bullet points and apply these consistently throughout your resume.

✔ Watch your verb tense (past tense for previous positions, present tense for current jobs). Fill your resume with keywords if you're sending it online. We discuss keywords in Chapter 4.

✔ Keep spacing between lines, words, paragraphs and headings the same.

✔ Spell out abbreviations and acronyms — particularly ones that aren't well known.

✔ Be consistent with punctuation. For example, check to see that you have placed full stops at the end of sentences and so on.

✔ Never shower your resume with graphics — unless, of course, you're applying for a role that requires you to demonstrate your creativity and design skills. Leave out amateurish clip art, too — this looks tacky and unprofessional.

✔ Put your name and page numbers in either the header or footer of your resume (in a smaller font), just in case your resume gets separated.

Don't type the words *resume* or *curriculum vitae* on the front page of your document. This is a waste of space and it's obvious what the document is called.

Listing with Bullet Points

Try to draw attention to specific parts of your resume by using bullet points. Bullets are a fantastic way to break up large paragraphs of text, and they're easy on the eye. Consider using short, sharp bullet points to list your responsibilities and achievements.

Filling Up with White Space

Cramming your resume with too much info makes it as appealing as entering a crowded lift. Fill your resume with plenty of white space to avoid suffocating the reader. Use single line spacing and set your top, bottom, left and right margins to around 2–2.5 centimetres (0.75–1 inches).

Getting Rid of the Glamour Shots

If you've got Hugh Jackman or Rose Byrne looks and you're thinking about wowing the recruiter with a photo of yourself, forget it. In case you've been hiding under a rock for many years, it's illegal for employers to discriminate when recruiting on the basis of physical appearance. Unless you're in the business of modelling, ditch the glamour shots on your resume and use your skills, abilities and qualifications to market your key assets.

Conversely, however, including a photo on a social media profile such as LinkedIn is highly recommended — but stick to a head and shoulders shot. A professional profile on social media is just as much about business networking as job hunting and, in business, we like to see who we are dealing with. Flip to Chapter 8 for more advice on creating a social media profile that supports your career aspirations.

Doing a Final Proofread

Okay. Time for some soapbox preaching. Always, and we repeat always, proofread and check your resume for spelling and grammar. Nothing is more of a turn-off for a recruiter than a resume chock full of typos — it's a good way to land yourself at the top of the rejection pile, especially if the role requires attention to detail.

Printing Like a Professional

Sending a hard copy of your resume is unusual these days, but if it's required then you want the best look possible. For a professional finish, you can use a laser printer or inkjet printer to produce copies of your resume, but always check your printouts prior to sending. Remember that streaks, blotches, smudges and faded lettering are definite no-no's. And, never print on both sides of a page.

Make sure your freshly printed resume is in pristine condition before you place it in the envelope. Is there more coffee on your resume than in your cup? Chances are you're not likely to create a good impression in a recruiter's eyes. Employers love clean, crisp, well-presented resumes.

Ditching the Display Folders

If you're hand delivering or mailing your resume to an employer, don't be fooled into thinking that display folders or binding will impress a recruiter. The sad fact is that the majority of presentation folders are pulled apart or filed in the round file — the bin. If you do post your resume, recruiters want to see it printed on white paper stapled in the top-left corner.

Avoid stapling the pages of your resume together if there's a strong chance your document may be scanned into a database. Instead, attach the document with a paper clip or, better yet, a bulldog clip.

Index

Notes

About the Authors

Amanda McCarthy began her career in teaching. She later went on to complete a Graduate Diploma in Human Resource Management and Industrial Relations at Griffith University, and an MBA from Queensland University of Technology.

Her study in Human Resource Management set alight her interest in the field of recruitment, which she has pursued with passion. This has resulted in Amanda having performed a variety of recruitment roles. She has worked in recruitment agencies, public and private organisations, and as a business owner specialising in professional resume writing and training.

Amanda delivered the Adult Community Education course 'Getting that Job' at Brisbane North Institute of TAFE. She has vast experience in presenting workshops to government employees that specifically focus on selection criteria, resume writing and interview preparation skills. Recognition of Amanda's expertise in the recruitment field is evidenced by the inclusion of her work on both the CareerOne and MyCareer websites, in the National Accountant journal and in the *Sunshine Coast Daily* and *Gympie Times* newspapers. In recent times, Amanda has been involved in a variety of careers-related projects.

Amanda is the author of *Australian Resumes For Dummies*, 1st edition, published in 2008. Amanda can be contacted at mccarthyaj@optusnet.com.au.

Kate Southam began her career as a journalist. Over more than a decade she wrote news and features for a number of newspapers and websites in Sydney, Hong Kong and London, including the *South China Morning Post*, *Sydney Morning Herald* and ninemsn.com.au. In October 1999, Kate was asked to become the Editor of News Corporation's first national employment website, CareerOne.com.au. In her 12 years in that role, Kate wrote a weekly column, *Ask Kate*, which was syndicated in more than 100 newspapers, and she authored the workplace blog, *Cube Farmer*, on news.com.au. She also became a regular commentator on career and workplace matters for radio and television.

Kate currently writes a number of columns and blogs and remains a regular on television and radio in Australia. She is also a career coach and a communications consultant.

Kate is a member of the Australian Institute of Management (AIM) and the Australian Chamber of Commerce. You can contact Kate via catherine.southam@bigpond.com or by visiting www.katesoutham.com.

Dedication

From Amanda: To all the unemployed job seekers out there ... *never ever give up on chasing your dreams*. This book is dedicated to you.

From Kate: I dedicate my work to my family, who have always encouraged me and cheered me on throughout my career from journalism to career and employment coaching, writing and commentary. Thank you so much for the support.

Authors' Acknowledgments

From Amanda: Firstly, I am grateful to my wonderful family who have always encouraged me to be the best I can be — my parents, Julie and Peter, sisters Nicole and Justine, brothers-in-law Greg and James and sister-in-law Ange. Special thanks go to my mentor Tom and my brother Murray for being an inspiration in my life.

To all my friends who have walked the *For Dummies* journey with me, thank you for your encouragement and support.

Most of all, this book would not have been possible without the hard work and dedication of the Wiley Publishing team, in particular Clare Dowdell, Kerry Laundon and Dani Karvess. Thank you all for your hard work getting the second edition onto the bookshelves and online. Thanks also to Kate for your amazing contribution to the second edition.

Finally a big thank you to all the HR professionals, career counsellors, recruitment agencies and search firms (too many to name individually) who contributed their time answering survey questions, providing general information and putting together sample resumes for the book.

From Kate: Thank you to the patient and encouraging team at Wiley, especially Clare Dowdell and Kerry Laundon. Thanks also to Lucy Sharp, Jonathan Greening of recruitment firm Hays and Andrea Swan for sharing their valuable knowledge about recruitment and employment.

I would also like to take this opportunity to thank all the people who have taught me so much about the world of work, particularly career coaches Max Eggert and Dawn Richards, and recruitment expert and career mentor Robert Godden. We all share a passion for empowering people and it has been my great fortune to have met you all. You've been extraordinarily generous.